RENEW YOUR MIND

Chantal Hofstee is a clinical psychologist and executive coach who works in the private, corporate and government sectors. She combines Cognitive Behavioural Therapy techniques with research-based mindfulness training to equip her clients with easy-to-use skills that train their brain and transform their lives. Through her companies Renew Your Mind and Renew Leadership, she and her team provide mindfulness and leadership courses and business training to enable people to take control of stress, improve focus and productivity and become better leaders. Find out more about Chantal at: www.renewyourmind.co.nz and www.renewleadership.co.nz.

RENEW YOUR MIND

How to rewire your brain
for a happier, healthier life

~

Chantal Hofstee

Clinical psychologist and executive coach

EXISLE
PUBLISHING

First published 2018

Exisle Publishing Pty Ltd
PO Box 864, Chatswood, NSW 2057, Australia
226 High Street, Dunedin, 9016, New Zealand
www.exislepublishing.com

A CiP record for this book is available from the National Library of Australia.

ISBN 978 1 925335 86 6

Designed by Enni Tuomisalo
Illustrations by Enni Tuomisalo
Cartoons by Jessie Miller
Typeset in PT Serif, font size 11pt, leading 18pt
Printed in China

This book uses paper sourced under ISO 14001 guidelines from well-managed forests and other controlled sources.

10 9 8 7 6 5 4 3 2 1

Note

The author would like to acknowledge the work of Jan Bernard, Pauline Skeates and Byron Katie.

Some of the material in this book was previously published in the author's earlier publication, *Mindfulness on the Run*. It has been fully revised and updated, and combined with new material here.

Disclaimer

This book is a general guide only and should never be a substitute for the skill, knowledge and experience of a qualified medical professional dealing with the facts, circumstances and symptoms of a particular case. The nutritional, medical and health information presented in this book is based on the research, training and professional experience of the author, and is true and complete to the best of their knowledge. However, this book is intended only as an informative guide; it is not intended to replace or countermand the advice given by the reader's personal physician. Because each person and situation is unique, the author and the publisher urge the reader to check with a qualified healthcare professional before using any procedure where there is a question as to its appropriateness. The author, publisher and their distributors are not responsible for any adverse effects or consequences resulting from the use of the information in this book. It is the responsibility of the reader to consult a physician or other qualified healthcare professional regarding their personal care. The intent of the information provided is to be helpful; however, there is no guarantee of results associated with the information provided.

To Pieter,

Thank you.

~

CONTENTS

~

INTRODUCTION:

Busy people

When was the last time you were not busy? How often do you feel stressed? Imagine that you could navigate your everyday life with a mind that is calm and focused and face your biggest challenges with courage and positive thoughts — what would be different?

Would you feel better? Stay calm when things don't go according to plan? Be more effective at work? Would your relationships be different? Would you be kinder to yourself?

It's easy to see stress as a normal part of life. But it does not have to be that way. I used to feel tired and stressed most of the time. My life felt like a never-ending race to do more, do better and tick the boxes on my to-do list, only to then add new things to it. Negative chatter and worries crowded my thoughts and I needed to achieve more and more to feel good about myself. All of this made it hard to be present and enjoy life.

I am grateful that those days are gone, and I have the Renew Your Mind techniques described in this book to thank for it.

These techniques are effective in reducing stress, and using them doesn't have to be difficult or time-consuming; you don't have to go away on a retreat or sit still for 20 minutes a day to calm your busy mind. Renewing your mind and training your brain can be simple and practical. In this book, I will show how you can achieve this not by changing what you do in everyday life but by changing how you do it. So you can enjoy a busy life without a busy mind.

The Renew Your Mind techniques described in this book are drawn from Cognitive Behavioural Therapy (CBT), research-based mindfulness and many other techniques that I have come across in my training and work as a psychologist. They have been combined and adapted to enhance efficiency without reducing effectiveness.

The main pillars of the Renew Your Mind techniques, however, are CBT and mindfulness, as research shows that both mindfulness and CBT effectively:

Reduce	Increase
Stress	Physical health
Anxiety	Emotion regulation
Depression	Productivity
Impulsivity	Overall wellbeing and happiness

CBT and mindfulness are two different ways to gain greater control of your thoughts which equals having greater control over your emotions, actions and their outcomes. The Renew Your Mind techniques changed me from a stressed and anxious over-committer to a content and mindful partner, parent and entrepreneur — and they could do the same for you.

This book will:

» Give you insights into the functioning of your brain.
» Help you understand the origins of your unhelpful patterns that cause stress.
» Teach you practical techniques that you can use in the midst of your busy everyday life.

Each chapter has been organized from broad (theory) to specific (how the theory relates to you personally). This has been done through exercises and sections called 'Insight inspiration' which contain questions that are designed to help you relate the theory to your personal life. This creates powerful insights and motivation for creating change through practising the suggested techniques that follow. You might want to use a notebook or journal to write down your answers.

To reach results more quickly and easily, I recommend the Renew Your Mind download. It has nine tracks with guided brain-training exercises you'll find in this book. This way you don't have to remember the steps; you just turn on the track of the technique you want to practise and hear my voice guiding you through the steps. Your practice couldn't be easier.

You can purchase the download from our website:
www.renewyourmind.co.nz

Today I am a clinical psychologist and executive coach. But I first discovered most of the techniques described in this book years ago, when I was a student. CBT and mindfulness techniques became a very effective stress-reduction toolkit through my university days. Years later, however, I found myself highly stressed, trying to juggle my roles as a partner, a parent and a director in a busy psychology practice. I just couldn't find the time to keep up my practice and keep my stress levels down, which led to a dilemma:

> You need mindfulness practice the most when you are busy and stressed, but during those times you cannot go on a retreat or set aside 20 minutes a day to meditate — you are simply too busy!

My life was not going to change any time soon, so I had two options: either give up practising mindfulness and the CBT techniques, or create a way of practising that would fit in with my busy lifestyle. This led me to develop the Renew Your Mind method: mindfulness and CBT techniques that are practical and highly effective, yet do not require you to sit still and meditate but instead can be done 'on the run'.

Let me share a real-life example of how I use the techniques on the go to combat stress. Just recently I was packing my things in the morning, and I had exactly 20 minutes before I had to leave the house. I was going to drop off my two-year-old son at his nanny's house and then calmly and mindfully make my way to the university where I was invited to lecture to a group of 32 students.

At the time, our house was being renovated, so we were staying with friends. As I was preparing for the day my son was watching a *Thomas the Tank Engine* DVD in my friend's beautiful home office. When all my things were packed, I went to get him — and found him drawing on her expensive, white office chair with a black marker. He could see the horror on my face and in an attempt to make me feel better he pointed at the drawing and said, 'Mama, Thomas the train!' I took a deep breath and suppressed the urge to scream *'NO!!!!!!'* I calmly took the pen away from him and said, 'Drawings on paper not on chairs, please.'

I tried to clean the chair with soap and water but the thick black stripes wouldn't come off. Then I remembered I had read that milk can help remove pen from fabrics, so I poured a tiny bit of milk on a cloth and tried to clean the chair, but with no result. So, I went to the kitchen again to try the soap one more time. At this point I was already 5 minutes late.

When I ran back into the office, I discovered that my son had emptied the entire bottle of milk on the white fabric chair! Half of the milk was on the chair and the other half had ended up on the beige woollen carpet. Before I knew it a loud 'No!' came from my mouth, which resulted in him crying as I rushed to the kitchen to get towels.

At this point I was 10 minutes late, had a crying child and a bottle of milk spilled on an expensive chair and carpet in my friend's home office. And there it was — the adrenaline and cortisol were kicking my stress response into gear. I could feel my breathing changing, my heart rate increasing and tunnel vision kicking in. Realizing that going into stress mode was not going to help me, I used the mindfulness technique called 'breath and senses' to calm myself down. For a few seconds I focused on my breathing and my surroundings to calm myself so I could make a plan. I called the nanny and asked her to come over and pick up my son. Then I comforted my son while trying to clean up the mess. When the nanny arrived I was 20 minutes late but I'd done the best I could to clean the mess. I jumped in the car and put the university address into my GPS system.

Then the thoughts came ... *What have I done? The milk is going to smell so bad. It will leave a big stain. My friend is going to be so upset!* Knowing that there is absolutely no point, or benefit, to stressing out, I calmed my brain down with mindfulness of the breath and senses: looking at the views, listening to the sounds and feeling the steering wheel, the pedals, the seat.

Feeling relatively calm again — knowing that I could still make it to the lecture on time — I noticed that the GPS had directed me somewhere unfamiliar. I stopped the car to check the address. Yes, I had put in the right address . . .

Ten minutes later I found myself in a part of town that was definitely not right. With just 5 minutes until the lecture was due to start I called the college to confirm the location and discovered I was 20 minutes away from it! Despair, frustration and pointless anger towards my phone kicked in. Again, I realized that this would not help me, it would only make me drive around like a mad woman, which isn't good for anyone. So, I used the beginner's mind technique to calm myself down again. I focused on the facts in a neutral, non-judgmental way: *I am in the car, driving to the college. The GPS took me to the wrong place, but I know where I am going now and the students will be informed I am on my way.*

This worked for a little while, until different thoughts started to creep in: *They are all going to think I am useless and that I don't care about being on time. They will never ever invite me back. No one will listen to my lecture. How can they take me seriously when I can't even manage to show up on time? And by the way, I have ruined my friend's carpet!*

My inner critic always picks excellent moments to show up! But I knew I could tackle it with the thought enquiry technique. After working through each of my stress triggering thoughts, asking myself *Can I be 100 percent sure that is true?*, I came to realize that none of them was. While my situation was not ideal, it was not the disaster my inner critic had tried to convince me it was.

When I finally arrived, I was calm again; to keep calm I was mindful of my posture, facial expressions and my breathing. The class was happy to see me, and I started my lecture with a story of stress.

'Just image that you are getting ready to deliver a lecture for a group of 32 students and your son is watching a *Thomas the Tank Engine* DVD while you are getting ready . . .'

This example shows that no matter how well you have trained your mind, you cannot eradicate stressful and challenging situations from your life; there is no escaping them. Training your brain with mindfulness and CBT is a way to train your brain to become better able to cope with these situations. It gives you a buffer that prevents your stressful thoughts or negative emotions from hijacking your brain and taking control.

CHAPTER 1:

Understanding your brain

When you want to make changes to the way you think and feel, it is important to understand the very thing that is making you think and feel: your brain. Your brain is your most important asset, a power station that connects your every thought, feeling and action. Yet people tend to take better care of their teeth, their hair and even their car than their brain. Understanding how your brain works helps you to take care of it and make it work better.

Your brain is made up mostly of water, about 10 per cent fats and 100,000 miles of blood vessels. The brain's basic building blocks are called neurons, and your brain has around 100 billion of them, each with between 1000 and 10,000 connections with other neurons. Information is passed along these connections through chemical messages and electrical impulses. These connections are called neural pathways and I will also refer to them as pathways or roads within the brain.

Neuroplasticity

Scientists used to think that the brain is fixed and hardwired by the time we become an adult. Research in only the past decade tells us that this is simply not true. The brain is flexible and changes throughout our lives, and this process is called neuroplasticity.

You can think of your brain as a dynamic power station, with many neural pathways that light up each time you think, feel or do something. The more a pathway is used, the thicker and stronger it becomes. This makes it easy for your brain's signals to travel that road. If you make a conscious effort to think, feel or do something differently, your brain begins to carve out a new road, which means a new pathway is established.

Brain training

Your brain is constantly changing and adapting based on your experiences. Changing old habits and creating new ones comes with directed and repeated practice of the new way of thinking, feeling and doing. By practising the Renew Your Mind techniques described in this book, you will literally rewire your brain. The techniques function as a circuit breaker that stops old, unhelpful patterns from being reinforced. They allow you to introduce and build new, more helpful roads. By doing this over and over again, the new pathways will become strong and take over. Eventually this new way of thinking, feeling or doing becomes second nature.

This process is not very different from physical exercise. Let's take push-ups as an example. Every single time you do a push-up you are changing something in the structure of your muscles. The more you practise, the stronger the muscles and easier the exercise becomes.

It takes six to eight weeks of daily practice for a new way of thinking, feeling or doing to form a strong new neural pathway. The good news is that even if you don't practise on a daily basis, you will start to notice changes within just a few weeks. The only requirement is that you do the exercises regularly.

The learning process has the following four phases.

PHASE	CATEGORY	OLD PATHWAY	NEW PATHWAY
1	unaware unskilled	existing	not existing
2	consciously unskilled	dominant	existing
3	consciously skilled	existing	dominant
4	unaware skilled	not existing	existing

Phase 1: Unaware unskilled

When you decide to start renewing your mind and training your brain, you are motivated to make changes. For most people at this stage, the desire to feel different is what drives them. When it comes to skills, at this stage you are unaware unskilled because you haven't yet been introduced to the techniques that allow you to train new skills. Your old pathways and habits are strong and no new pathways have been built — yet.

Phase 2: Consciously unskilled

In the early days of your practice, your brain begins to form new pathways. It requires effort and conscious attention for your brain to build and use these new pathways because the old pathways are still dominant and therefore easier to use. In this phase it can be a real challenge to keep practising!

Phase 3: Consciously skilled

After some weeks of doing the exercises you will notice that your practice becomes a lot easier. New pathways have been established and are strengthening. At some point the new pathways will become the dominant ones. But be aware — in times of stress, the old pathways can still take over quite quickly!

Phase 4: Unaware skilled

In the last phase of retraining your brain, the old pathways have become dormant. New pathways have become 'roads well-travelled'. Your practice is still important to keep the roads maintained, but you will notice the techniques have created a new way of thinking that now comes without conscious effort. You have become a more mindful person. At this point, a mindful way of thinking, feeling and doing has become second nature.

The green brain and the red brain

The way your perceptions, thoughts and emotions work and interact is quite complex. They are constantly changing and consist of many different layers. Some are part of your conscious mind, while others are part of your subconscious mind. At any given moment, when you peel away the different layers of thoughts and emotions all the way to the bottom of your subconscious mind, there are two options: your brain either feels safe or unsafe. Throughout this book I will refer to the unsafe state as the red-brain state and the safe state as the green-brain state. All of your thoughts, feelings and actions in that moment will come from either the safe (green) or unsafe (red) brain state.

There are various levels of safe or unsafe — you can picture this as a spectrum: at one end is the extremely safe green brain, and at the other end is the extremely unsafe red brain. Where your brain is on the spectrum depends on the situation, as well as your current thoughts.

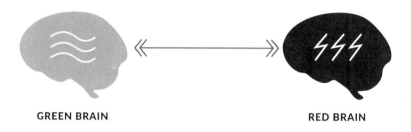

GREEN BRAIN   RED BRAIN

The red brain

The red-brain state is a state of stress. You can see the state of stress as a fire alarm. Stress is activated when the mind perceives a threat; this activates the fight-or-flight response. The fight-or-flight response makes you faster and stronger. I sometimes refer to it as 'the Hulk mode'. Having red brain available to us is actually very useful when there is a physical threat. Speed and strength are, after all, what keep you alive when you are faced with physical danger. When the fight-or-flight response kicks in, your brain and body are in the best possible state to deal with a threat, hence ensuring the greatest chance of survival.

The red brain can be triggered when there is no actual physical threat. Your brain reacts to how safe or unsafe you perceive a situation to be. Therefore, your thoughts are the most important factor in determining how your brain assesses a situation. For example, if you fear public speaking and say to yourself, 'I can't do this' or 'This will be a disaster', your brain perceives the situation as unsafe and the stress response is activated. In this state, the hormones cortisol and adrenaline are released, creating the following effects.

Physical effects:

» Tunnel vision
» Shallow breathing
» Stopped or slowed digestion
» Increased blood pressure and blood sugar
» Increased heart rate
» Suppressed immune system
» Tensed muscles

Psychological effects:

» Judgmental and black-and-white thinking
» Feeling stressed
» Narrow or fixed point of view
» Unkind manner
» Disconnection from others

» Loss of the ability to think creatively, be flexible and see other perspectives

The consequences of these effects include:

» Overlooking information

» Referring back to old patterns

» Poor decision-making and prioritizing

» Approaching problems with familiar solutions

» Miscommunications

» Decreased compassion and empathy

» Emotion-driven action rather than well-thought-through action

Having the Hulk mode available is essential for you to be able to deal with extreme situations — such as being attacked by a snake, running from a fire or seeing a child run onto the road. When you are running from a fire you need tunnel vision, tensed muscles, increased heart rate, blood pressure and blood sugar because these things ensure all the available energy goes towards speed and strength. On the other hand, the Hulk might be strong but he isn't very smart or considerate. Smart thinking and being kind and considerate are not priorities in red brain — you simply don't have time to think about how your grandmother is doing when you are running for your life! It is all about survival, and unnecessary functions — including your immune system, digestive system and higher-level thinking — are put on hold.

This is evident when we look at activity in the different brain areas while under stress. The brain can be divided into three main areas. The first area is the reptilian brain. This is the most primal part of the brain and it looks after the body's vital functions such as heart rate, breathing, temperature and balance. The next brain area is called the limbic system. This part of the brain looks after our emotions, motivation, memory and bodily functions such as appetite and sex drive. The third part of the brain is the neocortex, and this is the most developed part of the brain, responsible for higher-level thinking, speech and decision making.

Many studies have shown that stress leads to a dramatic loss of cognitive abilities by impairing the prefrontal cortex. Keep in mind that the brain is very complex and this is a simplification, but one could say that stress 'deactivates' most of the neocortex, leaving us with only about half of our brain active.

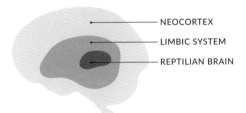

Looking at what stress does to our brain, it isn't hard to see that stress benefits us when we need speed and strength to deal with problems but it is not helpful at all when our problem is a deadline, a messy house or a difficult conversation. Almost all of our problems require our full brain to be active to help problem-solve and be strategic, but in a state of stress — red brain — our brain is blocked from being effective when we need it most.

Another reason the red brain should be reserved for emergency situations that require speed or strength is that spending too much time in the state of stress damages both your brain and the rest of your body. The stress response is designed to get you safely through extreme circumstances and then return to a state of calm. Once the snake has left, your system can calm down again. When the fire is put out the system can relax. The problem with stress caused by non-threatening situations is that there is often no calming down. When you are in the state of stress too often or stay there for too long, you risk ongoing negative physical consequences such as high blood pressure and heart failure, and psychological problems such as burnout, anxiety, depression and post-traumatic stress disorder. In less extreme cases, heightened stress leads to not being able to 'shut down' from work and constant worrying.

If you want to live a healthy and balanced life, the red-brain state does not have to be eliminated but should be reserved for emergency situations only.

The green brain

The green-brain state or, as I like to call it, 'the everyday brain', is on the opposite end of the spectrum. In this brain state the stress hormones cortisol and adrenaline are reduced and the 'relationship hormone' oxytocin is released, stimulating the following responses.

Physical effects:

- » Wide vision and flexible attention
- » Deep and slow breathing
- » Optimal digestion
- » Reduced blood pressure and blood sugar
- » Reduced heart rate
- » Optimal immune system
- » Relaxed muscles

Psychological effects:

- » Non-judgmental thinking
- » Feeling calm and in control
- » Seeing the bigger picture
- » Increased kindness and empathy
- » Feeling connected to others
- » Mental flexibility and perspective-taking

The consequences of these effects include:

» Improved health
» Eye for detail as well as the bigger picture
» Good decision-making and prioritizing
» Creative problem-solving
» Effective communication
» Improved relationships

Spending time in the green-brain state is essential for your physical health because it is in this state that your breathing, heart rate and blood pressure are able to find their natural base-rate levels. Essentially, your digestive system and immune system work at their best in this state.

In the green-brain state, all the resources in your brain become available to you and the smartest part of your brain, the prefrontal cortex, is fully engaged. High-level thinking, creativity and flexibility are unlocked and you are able to see the bigger picture and facts objectively. It is in this brain state that you can make good decisions and be truly effective and productive. In this state you will also be able to relax and process events and emotions. On top of that, the release of oxytocin immediately increases compassion, empathy and the desire to connect with others. This hormone is the fuel for our relationships and is essential for wellbeing.

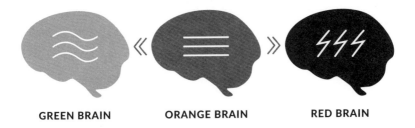

GREEN BRAIN   **ORANGE BRAIN**   **RED BRAIN**

The orange brain

The neutral, middle ground on the spectrum is the state of achieving, which I will refer to as the orange brain. This brain state is the 'go-go-go state', in which you plan and think about goals, and then set about working to achieve them. These goals can be big, such as building a house, or they can be small, such as simply posting a letter. This brain state is an area that falls between the green zone and the red zone on the spectrum. In this state you are telling your brain it will make it to the green zone once this or that task is completed. The orange brain does not have the negative symptoms of the red brain, nor does it have the benefits of the green brain. Because it is so goal-orientated, you can easily move from the orange to the red zone when something prevents you from reaching your goal.

It is important to keep in mind that these states fall on a spectrum, and we can move very quickly from one zone to another — sometimes within a split second! Also, there is nothing wrong with any of the brain states. Red, orange and green all serve their own purpose, and there is a time and place for each. Understanding how they affect your health, feelings and behaviour can be very useful because it helps make sense of how you live your life. The goal of CBT and mindfulness is not to block any of these states; it is to allow you to take greater control of the state your brain is in.

Productivity myth

Many people spend most of their time going back and forth between the state of achieving (orange brain) and the state of stress (red brain). Being aware and present (green brain) is reserved for after the work is done and special occasions like holidays, and is often associated with being lazy and unproductive.

This pattern makes sense because there is a small sub-state that is highly addictive and it is called success. When you reach your goal, the chemicals dopamine and serotonin are released, making you feel great. The sub-state of success can make it easy to get hooked into the pattern: achieving–stress–success. The problem with this pattern is that your happiness becomes tied to reaching your goals, instead of happiness coming from life in general. When your happiness is restricted in this way, it is fleeting and before you know it you are back in the stress or achieving state in order to reach your next goal and have your next 'hit' of fleeting happiness. This is an unsustainable pattern and ultimately leads to burnout, because we simply cannot function well without having enough green-brain time.

Research tells us that the belief held by many in this busy, modern world that stress increases productivity is simply not true. When you operate from a state of stress you are cognitively slower, waste more time, make more mistakes, overlook details and are less likely to perform well. You might feel as if you are doing well, but if you look at it objectively your performance is likely to be poorer than it would be if you were in the green-brain state. In a state of stress you might work harder, but in green brain you work smarter.

Working from a state of stress is like driving your car with the handbrake on: you might get from A to B, but it takes a lot of effort and in the long run it does damage.

Spending time in the green-brain state is not a luxury; it is the key to achieving optimal brain activity. Being in this brain state is incredibly healthy — reduced blood pressure and blood sugar, reduced heart rate, optimal digestion and immune system — and allows your body the opportunity to restore itself. Research shows that the green brain is also the ideal brain state for you to be effective and productive because you can see the bigger picture and have all your brain resources available to you, thus allowing your brain to function at its best. When you operate from this brain state you are at your most productive, effective, efficient, flexible and creative, so things seem to come more easily, sometimes even effortlessly.

Just think back to a time when you had a lightbulb moment, found a solution to a problem or had an idea that was truly innovative or a breakthrough of some sort. It is very likely that this idea, strategy or breakthrough came to you when you were in green brain. Perhaps you were in the shower, or walking in nature, exercising or about to fall asleep. One thing I know for sure, you didn't have a lightbulb moment when you were in red brain because your brain activity won't allow it and you probably weren't thinking hard on it either.

In green brain, while you are enjoying the moment, your smart brain is at work in the background, sorting information, making links, thinking innovatively and creatively and at some point this high-level thinking will enter your conscious mind, creating what we call an 'aha moment'. When you are doing green-brain activities that, on the surface, seem unproductive, your brain is highly productive. It doesn't go on a break as most people think; it is working for you in the background and it is working both on maintenance (processing and storing information) and engaging in high-level thinking, including creative problem-solving if you have given your brain that 'assignment'.

To further illustrate this there is fascinating research that shows us the very best way to tackle a difficult assignment or problem. According to this research, step one is to go through all the relevant information, allowing your brain to absorb it without yet asking your brain to do anything with that information. The next step is to pull out a pillow and take a nap. Yes, you read that correctly. According to research the best way to come up with brilliant ideas isn't to research more or to brainstorm. The best answer to a tough problem is to take a nap. While you are asleep (in green brain), your brain gets to work and processes, sorts and analyzes the information it has absorbed. Your brain connects that information to your experience and information stored in your memory and, while you are sleeping, engages in high-level thinking so that when you wake up the answers 'just come to you'. Even if you don't wake up with the perfect answer, you will see the situation from a different perspective and have a fresh, green-brain view on it. If you then ask yourself the simple question 'What would help?' or 'How can I fix this problem?' and notice what comes to mind, you will be able to come up with new, innovative and creative ideas that your red and orange brain simply are not able to come up with.

'I think 99 times and find nothing. I stop thinking, swim in silence, and the truth comes to me.'

— *Einstein*

Activating our green brain is by far the best chance we have of operating to the best of our ability, and the good news is that it is also the brain state in which we are the happiest. When we understand more about how our brain works it isn't hard to see that reserving green brain for after the work is done doesn't make much sense. You need your green brain in order to do your work effectively. Starting the day in green brain will give you much better outcomes than saving your green-brain activities until the end of the day.

Activating the green brain strategically

The goal of renewing your mind and training your brain is simply to achieve more green-brain time because, from green brain, health, productivity, improved relationships and happiness flow naturally. These are simply by-products or symptoms of green brain.

The first step to activating more green brain is to identify what circumstances (things, activities or environments) naturally activate your green brain and to be more strategic about using these natural triggers. Rather than saving all the green-brain triggers for the end of the day, ideally you schedule a few green-brain triggers at the start of your day and during your day. This will make it easier for you to stay out of red brain and have more green-brain time throughout the day.

For example, I start my day with an early rise (green-brain trigger for me) and morning run (another green-brain trigger) followed by cuddles with the kids (green-brain trigger) and then family breakfast (sometimes green) followed by a morning coffee (green-brain trigger).

During lunch, I always leave my desk and spend some time reading a book. The amazing thing I have found is that it is often during my lunch break, while reading a book, that the best ideas come to me. So, even though I'm not 'working', my brain is doing business and leadership strategy development in the background! Because of this, I always have a notepad with me to write down ideas that pop up during lunch.

Another helpful question to ask yourself is 'What are my red-brain triggers and is there any way I can reduce them or avoid them?'

For example, I avoid rushing by getting up early and not wasting time in the morning (avoids the red-brain trigger of rushing). I always put my keys in the same place (avoiding the red-brain trigger of not being able to find my keys), and my husband and I have a clear division of who does what in the mornings to make things run relatively smoothly (avoids rushing and irritation).

Often it is small preventable things that cause unnecessary stress (like not being able to find my keys) and activating green brain can sometimes be achieved through simple little things (like reserving 5 minutes each morning to cuddle with my kids).

Identifying your red- and green-brain triggers and then being strategic about them is the first step to having more green-brain time.

INSIGHT INSPIRATION: BRAIN TRIGGERS

1. List three red-brain triggers

    _____

    _____

    _____

    _____

2. List three green-brain triggers

    _____

    _____

    _____

    _____

3. How can I have more of the green-brain triggers?

    _____

    _____

    _____

    _____

    _____

    _____

4. How can I minimize or avoid the red-brain triggers?

    _____

    _____

    _____

    _____

    _____

    _____

Thoughts and the brain states

When there is a real physical threat, your system immediately moves to the red zone. However, there is another powerful trigger that can set off the red, orange or green brain: your thoughts. Your brain uses your thoughts as cues to determine how safe or unsafe a situation is, and based on this assessment it will activate one of the three states. Underneath all the rational thinking, your brain perceives worries and judgments as threats because they communicate to your brain that something is not right, and the brain then moves to the orange or the red zone.

For example, if you worry about your finances, the thought 'I don't have enough money' could come up. Your brain sees this thought as a signal for a potential threat and the red brain is activated. Your thoughts keep coming back to the perceived lack of money (fixed point of view) and you lose sight of the bigger picture of your financial situation, stopping you from prioritizing or coming up with creative solutions (poor decision-making). On a physical level, you might lose your appetite (slowed digestion), your breathing becomes shallow and your heart rate, blood pressure and blood sugar rise. Your brain and body are getting ready for fight-or-flight, even though there is no physical threat to run from. Your worries about money have then activated the red brain, making you much less able to effectively deal with any financial issues you might have.

It is important to realize that these brain states are linked to certain thoughts and brain activity; they are not directly linked to particular situations (except in the case of a physical threat). Following are some examples.

On your way to work

The red brain: You are getting ready to leave the house to go to work. You are rushing and feel frustrated. All you can think of is what you have to get done that day (fixed point of view); you are not present with what you do and because of this you forget to pack important things (overlooking things) and you cannot remember where you put your keys (lose sight of the bigger picture). When you hit the traffic, you become angry and annoyed with other road users (decreased compassion and empathy), and when you arrive at work you are feeling grumpy (negative mood).

The orange brain: You are getting ready to leave the house to go to work. You are focused on this goal (tunnel vision), and everything you do is linked to achieving it. You're keeping an eye on the time to make sure you stay on track. You are multitasking and thinking about work-related things in the meantime, telling yourself you can relax once the work day is over. When you hit the traffic (obstruction to the goal) you become restless and risk ending up in the red-brain zone.

The green brain: You are getting ready to leave the house to go to work. You are present in the moment while eating your breakfast (optimal digestion), getting dressed and packing your things (more efficient). While driving, you might listen to some music and notice things you see outside. When you hit the traffic, you accept this and don't let it ruin your mood. You are appreciative of the moment and can fully enjoy it in a relaxed way. You arrive at work in a good mood and are able to concentrate and work efficiently. You feel connected to your colleagues and are able to offer help and support when they need it.

Lying on the beach with a cocktail

The red brain: You are lying on the beach with a cocktail, feeling irritated by the heat, the temperature of the water and even the sand beneath your feet! You might be annoyed with the waiter for getting your order wrong, feeling disappointed with the hotel because it is not quite what you expected and angry because your children are too loud. You are lying on the beach with a cocktail feeling tense, restless and frustrated with what is happening around you.

The orange brain: You are lying on the beach with a cocktail, planning the rest of the day. You are thinking about all the sights you want to see, the activities you want to do and when you want to do them. You're there planning and organizing, and losing sight of all that is happening around you.

The green brain: You are lying on the beach with a cocktail, really being present in that moment: feeling the warm sun on your skin, the soft sand under your feet, hearing the sounds and watching your children play. Your breathing is deep, your heart rate is slow, and you are happy in this moment, just as it is.

The red-, orange- or green-brain states are all useful; they are simply designed for different purposes. Red deals with physical threats, green focuses on life in general, and orange is the middle ground. Learning how to be more in control of your thoughts will give you more control over the brain state you are in.

INSIGHT INSPIRATION: BRAIN STATES

1. What brain state are you in most of your time? Red, orange or green?

2. Can you identify how you move between the three brain states?

3. How has this pattern affected your life? (Think health, relationships, work, etc.)

CHAPTER 2:

Renew your mind with mindfulness

How can you renew your mind and train your brain to spend more time in the green-brain state and be more calm and present, as well as your most productive self? Mindfulness practice is one of the pillars of the Renew Your Mind approach to retraining your brain and learning how to 'switch on' this healthy, green-brain state. Before I show you how this works, let me first explain what mindfulness is and what it is not.

What is mindfulness?

Being mindful is a way of being in the world, which involves certain ways of thinking and paying attention. The definition of mindfulness is:

> Paying attention with kindness.

Mindfulness has two main components: attention and attitude.

Attention

Most people suffer from what is called a monkey mind. Your mind is like a monkey randomly swinging from branch to branch; your thoughts go from one thing to another, to another, to another. Before you know it, you are thinking about something and have no idea how you got there. The monkey mind often thinks about the past, pondering what happened or what you think should have gone differently. Or it thinks about the future, worrying about what might happen or thinking about all the things you have to get done. Unfortunately, most of us have a built-in tendency to have our thoughts wander off not to the nice and fun things of the past, nor the nice moments that are ahead. Instead, our thoughts tend to be drawn to the negative, thinking back to things that went wrong in the past or worrying about what might go wrong in the future. The monkey mind scans the past for regrets and the future for threats.

When your mind wanders to the past or the future you cannot be present with what is happening right now, which is a problem because the only thing that you can influence is the now. You cannot go back in time and change what has already happened, and who knows what the future holds? Your monkey mind is blocking you from being present in — and truly enjoying — the now. When you are not present with what is happening but thinking about other things, whether it is things of the past or the future, you are not able to effectively influence the present. Therefore, mindfulness is about taming the monkey mind and training your 'attention muscle' by regaining control of your thoughts by focusing on the now.

'An unstable mind is like an unstable camera:
you get a fuzzy picture.'

— *Christopher Germer*

This does not mean that you will never look back or plan ahead. It simply means that you will also be able to keep your attention on the present and you will be more in control of where your thoughts go. This puts you back in the driver's seat so that you — and not the monkey mind — decide where your thoughts go next.

Attitude

Being kind and non-judgmental is at the core of mindfulness practice. This means that you observe the facts of whatever situation you are in, without arguing with the facts or telling yourself things should be different. Taking the judgment out of your thoughts allows you to stay in green brain and avoid red brain; it allows you to keep your full brain engaged which will make you more effective in addressing or changing the situation. Staying kind and non-judgmental sounds simple, but when you start to practise mindfulness you will realize that you judge things, others and yourself all the time:

- » He shouldn't have said that.
- » You're wearing the wrong shoes.
- » The house looks horrible!
- » What a grumpy waiter.
- » My back hurts.
- » The dog is too loud.
- » Why can't I just focus?
- » That fence is so ugly.

As soon as you have a judgmental thought you send a signal to your brain that something is not right. This activates the orange or red brain and blocks the green brain. Mindfulness is about taming the inner critic, about erasing the *shoulds* and the *shouldn'ts* from your thinking and accepting everything as it is without arguing with the facts.

Remember, this does not mean that you stop making changes and just let everything be as it is. This is about training yourself to think in a way that reduces unhelpful stress so you can be more effective in reaching your goals. After a kind and non-judgmental thought, you can still decide to do something about a situation. Then you will be making changes from the ideal brain state rather than from a state of stress. It allows you to become *responsive* instead of *reactive*.

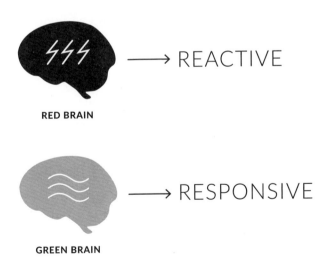

RED BRAIN

GREEN BRAIN

Here are some examples of judgmental thinking versus mindful thinking.

~

Judgmental thinking: He left his glass on the bench again! I am so sick of this, how many times do I have to tell him! How difficult can it be?

Mindful thinking: He left his glass on the bench. This is the way it is right now. How do I want to respond?

~

Judgmental thinking: My back hurts and it is so annoying! Why does this have to happen to me? It is so unfair.

Mindful thinking: I have a strong sensation in my back. This is the way it is right now. What would help?

~

Judgmental thinking: It is so rude and unprofessional of them to ignore my email. Argggghh, this is so annoying, it shows a complete lack of respect!

Mindful thinking: They are not responding to my email. It is what it is. How do I want to respond to this situation?

~

What mindfulness is not

There are four common myths about mindfulness.

1. Mindfulness is Buddhism

Mindfulness is often associated with Buddhism. However, mindfulness does not belong to any religion, culture or group. It has been practised by many different people in various cultures and religions and it has been called by many different names including meditation, centering prayer, contemplation or simply paying attention. Practising mindfulness is an inherent human capacity that is available to everyone.

2. Mindfulness is airy-fairy

Research-based mindfulness practice is based on a multitude of scientific studies and understanding of the brain. The number of scientific studies that have been done on mindfulness has increased drastically over the past few years and keeps growing. At the moment, more than 3000 scientific studies have been conducted on the subject, and most of them show positive results. However, not all of these studies have strong validity and a lot of improvements are yet to be made in the field of scientific research on mindfulness. Many of these studies and meta analyses can be viewed via the online database of the American Mindfulness Research Association (www.goamra.org).

3. Mindfulness is for hippies

You don't have to be even slightly alternative to practise mindfulness. In fact, even the corporate world has discovered that mindfulness is a stress-combat hero that increases creativity, innovation and productivity. No wonder businesses such as Apple, Google and Goldman Sachs are making mindfulness training available to their staff.

4. Mindfulness involves yoga

Mindfulness does not involve yoga or any other form of physical exercise. Mindfulness can be used during yoga or physical exercise but they are not the same thing. Mindfulness is about training your brain. There is no need for physical activity or challenging positions.

Self-compassion

When your thoughts become kinder and less judgmental something interesting happens: the way you relate to yourself changes. You grow in self-compassion and kindness towards yourself. Many people are incredibly harsh on themselves, constantly beating themselves up. This internal dialogue is a huge source of stress, but when you learn to be kind and non-judgmental towards yourself, you are reshaping your inner world and turning it from an unsafe place into a safe place. When your self-talk promotes green-brain activity instead of red-brain activity, you are doing your mind a huge favour by eradicating what might be the biggest source of stress you will ever have in your life.

When I stopped judging my husband for putting his glass on the bench instead of in the dishwasher, I was better able to address this recurring stress trigger (for me at least) in a calm and effective way. When I stopped complaining about my back pain and started my back exercises again, I found that it eased. When I didn't judge the lack of response to my email I could deal with it in a calm but assertive manner. You will be better able to reach your goals if you can keep your brain in the green zone or bring it back to a green-brain state before you respond. It may feel counter-intuitive, but when you practise present-moment awareness and kind and non-judgmental thoughts, you are increasing the likelihood of successfully making the changes you want to make.

'Mindfulness is brain manipulation
for a good cause.'

The power of mindfulness

As you start to practise mindfulness you are activating the green brain more and more. Everything you practise becomes stronger, so the more you activate the green brain, the stronger the green-brain pathways become and the easier it will be for your brain to access this state. This has a huge positive effect on both your physical and mental health.

Research shows that regular mindfulness practice does the following:

REDUCES	INCREASES
Stress	Compassion
Anxiety	Emotion regulation
Depression	Body regulation
Blood pressure	Productivity
Obsessive–compulsive symptoms	Enjoyment of food
Substance abuse	Self-compassion
Post-traumatic stress	General wellbeing
Impulsivity	Creative thinking
Inflammation	
Bipolar disorder symptoms	

Brain hygiene

Every time you do a mindfulness exercise you are taking care of your brain by building and maintaining green-brain pathways. You could call it brain hygiene. You brush your teeth a few times a day to make sure they stay healthy and strong and to prevent problems; practising mindfulness does the same for your brain. Mindfulness exercises give your brain a break from stress and make sure it stays healthy.

Mindfulness for improving focus

By focusing on what is happening right in front of you, in this moment, you are practising mindfulness. Focusing on your breath and your senses is a simple way to bring your attention back from the past or the future into the present moment.

You can practise this basic mindfulness technique anytime and anywhere. You don't have to sit still; you can practise while you are brushing your teeth, driving to work or riding the elevator. You can focus on your breath and senses when you are feeding the dog, doing the dishes or making a cup of tea. Sometimes even 10 seconds of focusing on your breath and senses is enough to reduce stress and reactivate the green brain. It does not matter when or how you practise this technique as long as you do it regularly. For your initial practice, I recommend you dedicate a particular moment each day to this brain-training exercise, and it often helps to tie your practice to something you are already doing. This way it is easier to remember to do it and you don't have to reserve extra time for it.

This technique comes easily to some people, yet it is hard for others. If you find your thoughts wandering off a lot, that's absolutely fine. Every single time you bring your attention back to your breath and your senses, you are practising mindfulness and training your attention muscle. In time, your attention muscle will become stronger and you will begin to find it easier to stay present and your thoughts won't wander off as much. A green-brain state is essential for effective learning and neuroplasticity, therefore it is important to keep a positive and non-judgmental attitude. Don't make your practice too hard. If you struggle practising for 5 minutes, then practise for 3 minutes. If practising for 3 minutes is hard, practise for 1 minute. Even 10 seconds of mindfulness is more effective than no mindfulness at all.

You can combine a daily practice with using the mindfulness technique to combat stress in the moment. When you are finding yourself getting stressed and moving towards the red end of the spectrum, pause and simply take a moment to focus on your breath and senses. Noticing your breath and noticing what you see, hear, physically feel, smell and taste, without judgment, instantly reduces stress, re-engages your cortex and moves you back into the green zone.

I begin most days with a mindfulness exercise. I take my fresh cup of coffee outside and I focus my attention on the present moment. In these 2 or 3 minutes I fully take in my surroundings. I feel the breeze on my skin, I listen to the birds and I notice my breathing. I also fully take in and enjoy my cup of coffee, by smelling it and tasting it with awareness.

These 3 minutes without distractions such as my phone or laptop help me to clear my head, centre myself and start the day in the green-brain state. To me this is the best possible start to each day.

EXERCISE 1:
MINDFULNESS OF THE BREATH

STEP 1. Focus on your breath.

STEP 2. Notice what it feels like to breathe in and out. Notice this without giving your opinion, or wanting to change anything. Simply feel the air and notice what happens in your body as you breathe in and out.

STEP 3. If your thoughts wander off, notice this. Then, in a kind and gentle way, bring your attention back to your breath.

 Tip: You can see your thoughts as butterflies or clouds that come and go. Just let them float past without engaging with them and turn your attention back to your breath.

EXERCISE 2:
MINDFULNESS OF THE SENSES

STEP 1. Focus on what you hear.

STEP 2. Observe and describe this, either in your mind or out loud. Do this in a kind, neutral and non-judgmental way, without labelling or giving your opinion. Simply describe the sounds that you hear.

For example, *I hear the clock ticking. I hear the birds singing. I hear the dog barking.*

STEP 3. Then focus on what you see.

STEP 4. Again observe and describe this in a kind, neutral and non-judgmental way without giving your opinion. Simply describe the sights that you see.

For example, *I see my desk. I see a tree. I see the light reflecting on the wall.*

STEP 5. Then focus on what you physically feel.

STEP 6. Observe and describe this in a kind and non-judgmental way. Simply notice and describe what you physically feel. If you feel any discomfort or tension, try to notice this without wanting to change it or fix it.

For example, *I feel the floor underneath my feet. I feel a sensation in my lower back (instead of I feel pain). I feel my clothing on my skin.*

STEP 7. Now focus on what you taste.

STEP 8. Observe and describe what you taste in a kind and non-judgmental way, without labelling or giving your opinion. Notice the subtlety of what you taste and where in your mouth you taste it.

For example, *I taste peppermint tea. I taste something sweet on the tip of my tongue. I taste a subtle salty taste on the sides of my tongue.*

STEP 9. Focus on what you smell.

STEP 10. Observe and describe what you smell without judging or giving your opinion. If you don't smell anything, then just notice that.

For example, *I smell a scented candle. I smell coffee. I smell nothing.*

 Tip: You can either do the full exercise, from step 1 through to step 10, or you can choose to focus on only some of your senses. The order in which you do this is irrelevant. I recommend that you try all of them and then keep using the ones you find most calming and centring.

RENEW YOUR MIND TIP

Put your commute time to good use by spending a few minutes focusing on your breath and senses on your way to work.

CHAPTER 3:

Navigating emotions

Have you ever wondered why some people always seem to have a positive outlook on life regardless of challenges and disappointments? And why others, who seem to have it all, worry and are unsatisfied and judgmental?

Your base-rate happiness is partly determined by your situation and partly by several other factors, one of which is your personality. Some people are naturally resilient and have a more positive outlook than others. Another factor is your upbringing. How did your parents handle negative events? What sort of response did they model? It is likely that your way of responding to negative emotions is somewhat similar. Your coping mechanisms, the strategies you use to manage internal or external stress, also impact how you process negative events and emotions. Lastly, your thoughts influence whether unpleasant emotions come and go as a natural result of events or become 'stuck' and taint your experience of everyday life.

There are four basic emotions that humans can experience:

» Anger

» Fear

» Happiness

» Sadness

All the other emotions that we experience fall under one of these four categories. For example, nervousness falls under fear, irritation falls under anger, and cheerfulness falls under happiness.

People often associate emotions with words like 'uncomfortable', 'messy' and a lack of control, and it seems terribly unfair that three out of our four basic emotions are unpleasant ones. However, emotions are nothing more than chemical messages produced by your brain to communicate something to you. Not all emotions are pleasant but all emotions serve an important purpose. If humans did not experience any fear we would have become extinct a long time ago. Fear stops you from taking risks and doing things that could harm you. Anger is a signal that someone is overstepping your boundaries and that you need to intervene. Sadness also signals that something is not right; maybe you have lost something or someone important to you. Feeling happy indicates that things are going well and you are enjoying the people or things around you.

Your emotions are not there to make your life harder; your emotions are in part designed to be your internal GPS system. They are the 'voice' that draws your attention to whatever your brain thinks needs your attention and then informs your decision-making. For example, when you feel exhausted, it is simply your body telling you that you have too much on your plate and you need to reorganize your schedule and rest more. When you feel annoyed with your partner, it is your brain telling you that you need to make time to properly connect with each other and discuss the issues causing the annoyance. When you feel disrespected by your children, it is your brain communicating to you that their behaviour is unacceptable to you and you need to be firmer with your boundaries.

Just as a smoke alarm signals to you that there is a situation in need of your attention, your emotions signal to you that there is a situation in need of your attention. Yet many people are in a never-ending battle of fighting the signals, of wrestling with their emotions. As a result, they don't address the issues their brain is trying to direct them to through the emotion, which results in the volume of the emotion being turned up even more in an attempt to achieve this.

'The word happiness would lose its meaning if it were not balanced by sadness.'

— Carl Jung

When we can accept our emotions without judging them or trying to change them or fix them, we can listen to what they are telling us and choose how we respond. In this way, our emotions become our internal GPS system. When the emotions are met with a kind and non-judgmental listening ear (as you will learn to practise in the technique at the end of this chapter) they will usually simply defuse. It is when we disregard our emotions, or meet them with criticism or judgment that they become stuck and turn into messy, unruly things that seem determined to make our life hard.

Green brain is often confused with an absence of fear, sadness and anger, but there is nothing wrong with experiencing any of these emotions; they are all valid and real and each of them communicates something important. The green-brain approach to emotions is to accept them, validate them and listen to what they are there to tell you. When you approach emotions this way, you can remain in green brain and *respond* to them rather than *react* out of emotion-driven impulse. Noticing your emotions with kindness avoids the emotions taking control and triggering you into red brain. In green brain you can choose how you respond; in red brain emotions hack your reactions.

The emotional balloon

We can think of our emotions as an emotional balloon with four openings.

HAPPINESS   ANGER

SADNESS   FEAR

As we go through life, things happen and our emotions are stirred. The pressure in the balloon builds. When enough pressure builds up it needs to be released and it will come out through one of these four openings. The pressure can be released through anger, sadness, fear or happiness.

Young children have all the openings of their emotional balloon wide open, which is why they can experience intense anger, sadness, happiness and even fear in a matter of minutes. The healthiest option is to keep all the openings accessible, but as you grow up, some of these openings can become partially or even completely closed. Which openings remain fully open and which become partially or fully closed depends on your personality, the culture you grew up in, significant life events and your upbringing. The extent to which the four openings are open becomes a blueprint for your emotional landscape as an adult. Closing off one or more openings leads to unbalanced reactions because the pressure cannot be released through the appropriate funnel. It builds up and then is redirected to come out through an alternative emotion. Here are some examples.

Upbringing

A boy grows up in a family where he is taught that boys don't cry. He learns to see sadness as a sign of weakness, and therefore he completely or partially closes off the opening of sadness.

HAPPINESS   ANGER

SADNESS   FEAR

A girl grows up with an anxious mother who constantly expresses her worries and shows very little happiness. The

opening of fear becomes wider and wider as this little girl grows up and happiness becomes smaller.

HAPPINESS   ANGER

SADNESS   FEAR

A boy grows up in a family with many struggles; to not be a burden to his parents he adopts the role of the happy child. The opening of happiness becomes wide and the other three become partially or completely closed off.

HAPPINESS   ANGER

SADNESS   FEAR

Personality

An introverted person is more likely to partially or completely close off the 'bigger emotions' — anger and happiness — and to leave open the 'smaller emotions' — fear and sadness. The opposite tendency is likely for an extroverted person.

Significant life events

Significant life events are events including traumas that at the time or afterwards were experienced by the person as significant and are often accompanied by a strong emotional response combined with a lack of control. Events such as losing a loved family member or suffering any type of abuse (physical, emotional or sexual) are always significant events. Events don't always have to be significant for everyone in order to have a deep impact on a child. For example, losing their teddy bear or being frightened by a fire alarm in the absence of parents can be significant events.

A young boy is overwhelmed by fear when the fire alarm goes off while he is with a babysitter. She is unable to calm him down. The opening of fear becomes enlarged and the opening of happiness becomes partially or fully closed.

HAPPINESS   ANGER

SADNESS   FEAR

A girl is emotionally and verbally abused in her childhood; sadness and fear become wide open, and happiness becomes partially or completely closed off.

HAPPINESS   ANGER

SADNESS   FEAR

A boy is humiliated by his father when he receives a bad grade in school; both fear and anger become enlarged, and happiness and sadness become smaller.

INSIGHT INSPIRATION

1. Take a moment to think about your emotional balloon. Which openings are fully open and which ones are partially or completely closed off? It can help to think of the emotions you feel on a regular basis (open) and the ones you hardly ever feel (closed).

    _____

    _____

    _____

    _____

    _____

    _____

2. What consequences has this emotional blueprint had for you?

    _____

    _____

    _____

    _____

    _____

3. How has this affected your life and your relationships?

    _____

    _____

    _____

    _____

    _____

    _____

The conscious and the subconscious mind

Your brain requires a lot of energy to operate, so it seeks to conserve energy by using efficient ways of operating. One way it does this is through conscious and subconscious processing. To save brain energy, the brain automates much of what you do, and these become the subconscious processes. Your brain's subconscious processes take care of basic life functions, such as breathing, heart rate and digestion.

The subconscious brain takes care of the fight-or-flight response (stress levels) and learned behaviours and habits. This way you don't have to pay attention to these things; they happen on autopilot. Up to 95 per cent of all processes happen at the subconscious level — and this is a good thing! If all these processes were overcrowding your conscious mind, your system would simply overload.

You can think of your mind as an iceberg, with the conscious mind being the part above the water and the subconscious mind the part below the surface.

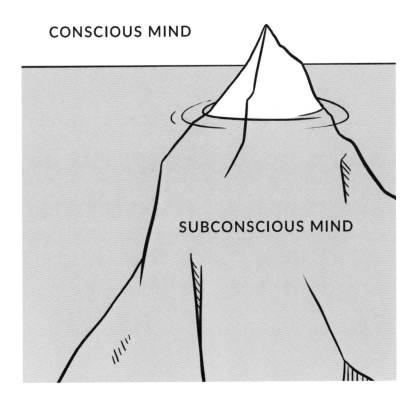

CONSCIOUS MIND

SUBCONSCIOUS MIND

The conscious mind

The things that happen in your conscious mind are the things you are aware of right now, in this moment. Your conscious mind has limited capacity and you can compare your awareness to a spotlight that moves from one thing to another. For example, if you are paying attention to what you are reading, then your present moment awareness is focused on the text of this book. If you become distracted by a sound your awareness moves from the text to the sound.

If you are distracted by worries your awareness is with the worries rather than the text.

The subconscious mind

The subconscious mind can be divided into two parts. The first part is just beneath the surface and includes all the things that you can relatively easily bring to mind. You can think of it as a library: there are many books but you won't read them all at once. If you need certain information you know where to look for it and you are able to find it and bring it into your immediate consciousness.

The lower part of your subconscious mind consists of the processes that occur automatically and are not readily available for introspection. These include thought processes, memories and feelings. You can think of your subconscious mind as a messy basement with many unopened boxes. They have been stored there a long time ago and you are unaware of what is in them. Even though they exist under the surface of your conscious awareness, these processes can impact your conscious thoughts, feelings and behaviours, especially when you are in red brain.

Emotions

Now, back to emotions.

When you experience an emotion, there are three options. The emotion can:

» become stuck

» be suppressed or

» be processed.

Stuck in emotions

When emotions become stuck, you cannot move on from whatever experience triggered that emotion; both your brain and your body remain in an upset state. You know you are stuck in an emotion when you cannot stop thinking about the event that triggered it and you stay emotionally upset for days or even weeks or months (even if this is on and off). Most of us have experienced this at some stage, and when this state lasts for a long time, serious problems can occur. Being stuck in emotions is accompanied by an overactive red brain and increases the risk of developing depression, anxiety, issues with sleeping and post-traumatic stress disorder.

Post-traumatic stress disorder is an example of a brain becoming stuck on an event and the emotions it has triggered. In this state the person can experience:

- » random flashbacks
- » nightmares
- » continuous high stress levels
- » tensed muscles
- » low mood
- » agitation
- » fear of returning to the place the event happened
- » changed sleep patterns
- » changes in appetite.

Here are some examples.

- » Your partner just ended the relationship. You cannot think about anything else. You lose your appetite, have trouble sleeping and lack motivation to do anything. You have random flashbacks to the good and the bad times. In your mind you replay the conversations you had countless times without gaining any new insights or resolutions.
- » Someone said something unkind to you and you cannot stop thinking about it. Every time you think back to what happened you feel tense, there is a knot in your stomach and you get upset. Rather than helpful thinking, your thoughts just keep repeating what happened, making you feel more and more upset.

When we respond to our emotions by judging them, trying to change them or 'fix' them, we are interfering with our brain's natural ways of processing the emotion. Emotions are likely to become stuck when they are not allowed to finish their 'full cycle' and are therefore not processed.

Suppressed emotions

The second option we have when it comes to emotions is to suppress them. Most people don't like to pay much attention to negative emotions. This can be because you are being hard on yourself ('Don't get upset, it was your own fault!'), or because you think paying attention to the emotion will make it worse instead of better ('Just get over it, it's no big deal'), or because you have to keep going and don't have the time or opportunity to allow your attention to dwell on your feelings ('I don't have time to be upset, I have a deadline!'). This will lead to suppressing the emotion, which might work in the short term but leads to stress either in the moment or afterwards.

Think back to your emotional balloon and the openings that are partially or completely closed off. The emotions that you have learned to close off do not just disappear; they are transported from the conscious mind to the subconscious mind. You can compare suppressing emotions to pushing a balloon under water: it requires energy, and in time the balloon will just pop up again. The same thing happens with suppressed emotions: they find their way into your thoughts and feelings and are often expressed in messy ways.

Here are some examples.

» A colleague gives you negative feedback. You keep your frustration in but when you go out for coffee you are unfriendly to the waitress.

» A mother is frustrated by her child but tries to stay calm and patient. Then her husband comes home and she yells at him over something minor.

» A child feels intimidated by his new baby brother but is told that he has to be nice to him. He then starts to hit other children.

» Your employee is not doing a good job. You worry about confronting him but try not to think about it. You go home but instead of engaging you disconnect and withdraw from your partner.

Processing emotions

The third, and preferred, option of dealing with emotions is to process them. When you process an emotion your brain works through what happened, then stores the information in the library of your brain in a neat and orderly way. Then the event becomes a memory. It might be an unpleasant memory, but when you think back to it you feel mostly calm and remain in control of your thoughts and feelings. All events and emotions can be processed, no matter how horrible they are. Significant events like traumas often take more time to process than small events, but they can be fully processed and then stored in the mind's library.

I believe that being equipped to allow this process to happen — rather than responding to emotions by immediately trying to change them, fix them or work them out — is an important pathway to emotional health and resilience. It allows us (and those around us) to experience first-hand that emotions, no matter how uncomfortable they are, will pass and we will feel all right again.

Allowing yourself to feel your feelings without judgment or being in a hurry to make them disappear has important healing qualities and allows us to develop a stable sense of self that doesn't change whether we feel momentarily angry, sad or anxious. Feeling the feeling 'all the way to the end' allows our brain to deal with it effectively so that we can really recover and move on afterwards rather than moving on too quickly and being left with lingering emotional residue.

People often think that allowing themselves to feel an emotion with kindness will lead to the emotion getting stuck or to them feeling overwhelmed. Usually the opposite is true. When you allow an emotion to be there, responding to it with kindness and responding to the situation it's trying to attract your attention to, the emotion will defuse faster and you are more likely to take healthy action as a response to the situation that triggered it.

Emotions truly are like waves: you can learn to become a skilled surfer and the waves will come and go without throwing you off balance. The more you fight them the more likely it is that you will get sucked into red-brain emotional messiness and chaos.

The green brain promotes the processing of emotions while the orange- and red-brain states promote suppressing or becoming stuck in emotions. It is important to realize that you can experience an unpleasant emotion and still be in the green-brain state. The green- or red-brain activity is determined by how you approach the emotion. You can be green-brain angry, green-brain upset, green-brain anxious and green-brain sad. If you approach the emotion with a kind and non-judgmental attitude you remain in the green zone where processing can take place and you can stay in control of your actions. When you judge your emotion you move to orange or red and processing is blocked, leaving only the options of suppressing or becoming stuck.

Acknowledge–Link–Let Go

The approach to mindfully processing emotions proposed by therapist Pauline Skeates states that the brain requires three steps to process emotions. The first step is to acknowledge the emotion, the second step is to link the emotion to the trigger, and the third step is to let the emotion go.

Step 1: Acknowledge

Your brain cannot process something that you do not acknowledge. In order to be processed, an event and the emotion attached need your kind and non-judgmental attention. This attitude is required to ensure the green-brain state, which is necessary for processing to happen.

One way of acknowledging your emotion is by simply saying 'hello' to it.

Hello feeling nervous.

Hello anger.

Hello stress.

Saying hello to an emotion is a kind and non-judgmental way of acknowledging it and activating the green brain. This process 'separates' you from the emotion, which immediately gives you a different perspective and more control through activating green brain. It reminds you that you are not consumed by this emotion. You are you, and this emotion is a temporary feeling that is here, in this moment. You are not anger; there is you, and you are saying hello to anger. You are not stress; there is you, and you are acknowledging that in this moment the wave of stress is also there.

'The more comfortably you can acknowledge and accept your emotions the easier they can be processed and diffused.'

— *Pauline Skeates*

Step 2: Link

The second step in processing an emotion is to *link* it to the event that caused it. In other words, you are responding to the internal smoke alarm by examining what has set it off. Thus, the emotion has fulfilled its purpose and now that your attention is focused on what your brain is 'warning' you about, it can 'turn down the volume' of the signal (the emotion). An easy and effective way to make this link is to say to the emotion: 'It makes perfect sense that you are here, given the situation.'

When you say this, either out loud or in your mind, your brain immediately starts to make sense of why that emotion is there. It starts to scan your memory to look for the triggers that caused the emotion, and in this way your attention is brought to these triggers in a calm and non-judgmental way. Give yourself a moment to notice the things that come into your awareness, without judging them or trying to make them any different. Simply notice what comes to your mind and observe these things in a kind and non-judgmental way. By doing that the linking is done.

Once you start to practise this skill you will gain important insight into what is triggering your emotions. You can take the linking one step further by saying to the emotion: 'It makes perfect sense that you are here, given what I have gone through.'

There are often underlying, unprocessed events that are fuelling your current emotion without you realizing it. When you say to the emotion, 'It makes perfect sense that you are here, given what I have gone through,' your brain automatically begins to scan your past for these underlying, unprocessed events. Memories will come up, creating sometimes surprising insights and uncovering links you were not aware of. This often leads to the response, 'I had no idea that past event was linked to why I am feeling this way, but now I see it makes so much sense.'

For most people, gaining insights into links between current emotions and past events gives immediate relief and understanding. This helps in applying the next step.

Step 3: Let go

The last step of processing emotions is letting go. When you let go you are not saying that what happened was okay or that you will let it happen again. You are letting go of the emotions so your brain can store them in the library of your mind and you can move on or respond to the trigger effectively.

To let go:

» Put one hand on your chest and one hand on your stomach.

» Take a deep breath.

» As you breathe out, relax and drop your shoulders.

» Say or think, 'I let it go.'

» Repeat a few times.

Your emotions and physical body are manifestly connected. When you think back to something you have not processed, it will lead to tension in your neck and shoulder area, and your breathing will become shallow. When you consciously take deep breaths and relax your shoulders, you are adjusting your physical body to resemble green-brain posture (relaxed muscles) and green-brain breathing (slow, deep breaths). Because your brain and the rest of your body are connected, your brain will respond to the green-brain posture and breathing by activating the brain state that corresponds to this: green brain. When green brain is activated your mind can process the emotion and let it go.

You can increase the impact of this step by placing one hand on your chest and the other hand on your stomach. When you do this something extraordinary happens in your brain: what we call the social engagement system is activated. This is a combination of brain areas that become active in meaningful social interaction. By placing one hand on your chest and one on your stomach, you are activating the same brain activity that is activated when you are holding the hand of a loved one.

Research shows that when the social engagement system is activated, people feel more secure and confident. They also assess situations as less challenging. By adding this simple step to the Acknowledge–Link–Let Go (ALL) technique you are offering yourself emotional support and encouragement, as well as increasing your green-brain activity and the effectiveness of the exercise.

Step 4: What would help?

Now that the emotion is processed and you are in green brain, this is the perfect time for creative problem-solving. Simply ask yourself, 'What would help?' or 'What small step can I take to make this situation better?' This will often lead to a fresh perspective and new strategies to tackle the problem or situation that triggered the emotion.

What if Acknowledge–Link–Let Go doesn't work?

Some emotions are processed after doing this exercise only once. Others take more time. This often depends on how strong the emotion is. Every time you do this exercise you are taking a step in processing the event and emotion.

What if it triggers another unpleasant emotion?

With more significant events you will often find that once you have processed one emotion you may encounter another. When you do, just repeat the steps with this new emotion that has come to your awareness. Once you feel calm and peaceful and can look back at what happened without your emotions being stirred again, you have fully processed the event and the emotion.

Here are some examples.

Linking to the situation

Stuck in stress (red brain): Jenny is running late and feels stressed. She thinks to herself, 'What is wrong with me, why can't I ever be on time?! I am definitely going to be late now. I can't believe it, I am so bad at planning!' She feels stressed, her breathing is shallow and her muscles are tense.

Processing stress (green brain): Jenny is running late and feels stressed. She says to the emotion, 'Hello stress. It makes perfect sense that you are here, because I am late and I hate being late.' Then she breathes out, drops her shoulders and says, 'I let it go.' Her breathing becomes deeper, her muscles relax and she feels calm and in control again.

Stuck in anger (red brain): Dan is confronted by his boss in an inconsiderate way. He thinks, 'This guy is such an arrogant bastard, he doesn't even know what he's talking about!' He feels angry, his breathing becomes shallow and his muscles are tense.

Processing frustration (green brain): Dan is confronted by his boss in an inconsiderate way. He processes his anger by thinking, 'Hello anger. It makes perfect sense that you are here. My boss's behaviour is making me angry, and it's a repeat of past occasions when he has acted in the same way.' He then breathes out, drops his shoulders and tries to let go of the anger. After repeating this a few times he feels calm and in control again. When he asks himself, 'What would help?' he can come up with helpful, assertive ways to address the situation.

Linking to the past

Stuck in frustration (red brain): Katherine becomes very frustrated when her partner does not respond quickly enough when she asks him something. She thinks, 'Why is he not listening when I speak to him? It is so disrespectful!' This makes her feel even more frustrated and she shouts, 'Why don't you listen to me!' An argument is the result.

Processing frustration (green brain): Katherine becomes very frustrated when her partner does not respond quickly enough when she asks him something. She says to herself, 'Hello frustration, it makes perfect sense that you are here, given what I have gone through.' Then the memory of her father often ignoring her comes into her mind and she realizes that her intense frustration with her partner is fuelled by the buried frustration of being ignored by her father. She takes a few deep breaths, relaxes her shoulders and lets it go. When she has calmed down she reminds herself that her partner is not like her father. This makes her want to connect to her partner instead of becoming angry.

Stuck in insecurity (red brain): Alex becomes filled with self-doubt at work and feels nervous and insecure at meetings. He thinks, 'I don't have the right skills to do this job, I am such a failure and will let everyone down.' His self-esteem and mood quickly drop, negatively impacting his ability to think and perform. When he comes home all he thinks about is work and he isolates himself from his family more and more.

Processing insecurity (green brain): Alex becomes filled with self-doubt at work and feels nervous and insecure at meetings. He thinks, 'Hello insecurity, it makes perfect sense that you are here, given what I have gone through.' Memories of his demanding father telling him he was a failure when he did not excel come to his mind. He takes a deep breath, drops his shoulders and thinks to himself, 'I let it go. I don't have to please my father anymore and I am not a failure.' His system calms down, he regains his focus and does not give in to the feeling or the need to work until late in the evening but instead he spends quality time with his family.

A green-brain approach to emotions

Emotions are not always pleasant or comfortable but they are important because they are part of your brain's messaging system. When you suppress emotions you miss the message your brain is giving you. When you become stuck in an emotion you react out of an emotion-driven impulse, which often does more harm than good. But emotions don't have to automatically put you in the orange or red zone — luckily there is a green-brain alternative. A green-brain approach to emotions is to process them by taking them seriously and listening to them. When you process the emotion your system calms down and activates green brain, allowing you to effectively respond. In this calm, mindful state you can see clearly and you can actually address the situation in a healthy and effective way.

> Processing emotions moves you from reactive to responsive.

EXERCISE 3:
FEELING BETTER

STEP 1. Turn your attention to the emotion you are feeling.

STEP 2. Say 'hello' to the emotion.

For example, *Hello stress. Hello feeling small. Hello being upset.*

STEP 3. Tell the emotion: 'It makes perfect sense that you are here, given the situation.'

STEP 4. Take a moment to notice what comes to your mind. Stay kind and non-judgmental as you do this, allowing anything that comes to your mind, welcoming it and noticing it, without trying to change it or figure it out.

STEP 5. Put one hand on your chest and one hand on your stomach.

STEP 6. Take five deep breaths. As you breathe out, relax your shoulders and say to yourself: 'I let it go.'

STEP 7. Notice what you are becoming aware of.

 RENEW YOUR MIND TIP

This technique works for processing emotions as they arise, as well as after the fact. Just think back to the situation that upset you and follow the same steps.

CHAPTER 4:

Green-brain connection

Feeling connected to others is at the core of happiness. Your brain is wired to want and seek connection with others because this connection provides safety on many levels. But relationships can be challenging and we often become emotionally disconnected from the ones we love; all it takes is a bit of stress, a busy agenda or a misplaced comment. When you become disconnected from the people you love, it greatly affects your happiness and theirs.

You can be in a room full of people but feel completely disconnected, or you can be all by yourself yet feel incredibly connected to the people in your life. Connection is not being around people, it is feeling that someone cares about you. In this chapter we will look into how green-brain techniques can be applied to communication and how you can use mindful communication to avoid emotional disconnection and strengthen your bond with the people you love most.

Communication

You are practising mindfulness when you pay attention to what is happening and you observe it in a kind and non-judgmental way. When you apply this to social interaction it means being present with other people, accepting them and their experience as it is for them, in that moment.

As researcher Brené Brown beautifully puts it in her message on empathy versus sympathy: 'Theresa Wiseman, a nursing scholar, researched empathy and came up with four qualities of empathy. The first one is perspective-taking, the ability to take the perspective of another person or recognize *their* perspective as *their* truth. This involves avoiding judgment, which is not easy when you enjoy it as much as most of us do, and recognizing emotion in other people and then communicating that.' Brown describes empathy as a sacred space and a dynamic that fuels connection. The opposite of empathy is sympathy. Sympathy fuels disconnection even though it often comes from good intentions. Sympathy is when someone shares something with you that is incredibly painful and you respond with the words 'at least'.

'I had a miscarriage . . .'
'At least you know you can get pregnant.'

'John is being kicked out of school . . .'
'At least your daughter is an A student.'

'My marriage is falling apart . . .'
'At least you have a marriage.'

We do this all the time. We try to make people feel better by redirecting their attention to more positive things. The truth is, it doesn't work. Failing to acknowledge their emotions merely fuels disconnection. Empathy, or connection, happens when you learn to accept other people's uncomfortable emotions; when you stop trying to fix them but create space for whatever they are feeling in that moment. Connection is not trying to pull the other person out of the darkness they are in; it is climbing down and joining them in their experience, knowing that this too shall pass.

This does not mean that you should never try to cheer anyone up or that you should not give advice. It also does not mean that because you accept their feelings you also have to accept all of their behaviour. You can still address things, but if you first connect, then whatever you do after that will have more effect.

	GREEN BRAIN	RED BRAIN
Underlying constructs	Safe In control/calm	Unsafe Fight-or-flight/stress
Observations	Open view Taking perspective	Fixed point of view Only see your own perspective
Attitude	Kind manner Open	Unkind manner Closed
Thinking	Non-judgmental Seeing details/nuances	Judgmental Black/white
Risk of conflict	Low	High

Let me refresh your memory regarding the red brain and the green brain. As you can see in the table above, a brain in the green zone feels safe and therefore calm and in control. This brain state allows you to see details and nuances and allows you to take another person's perspective. The green brain promotes a kind manner and non-judgmental thinking, which leads to a low risk of conflict. At the opposite end of the spectrum is the red brain. A brain in the red zone feels unsafe. This activates the stress (fight-or-flight) response, putting the brain and body in the best possible state to run or fight but the worst possible state to communicate. In this state a fixed point of view is activated; you only have eyes for the thing that is causing you stress, with no room in your mind for anything else. Taking someone else's perspective becomes hard, if not impossible. Your thinking becomes black-and-white and you are likely to adopt an unkind and judgmental attitude. Until the other person has moved out of the red zone, communication is usually ineffective. Someone who is in red brain won't be able to take on board much of what you have to say.

Very often people in a relationship want the exact same thing, whether it is a love relationship, a parent–child relationship or a work relationship. Both parties need to be heard, to be acknowledged and to have their emotions validated. These are the core principles of connection. Why? Because making someone feel heard, acknowledged and validated is a powerful way to activate their green brain. Because connection meets these needs it automatically moves the other person's brain out of the red zone. Creating a safe space for their emotions helps defuse them so quickly that you will see the person changing within minutes, sometimes even seconds.

Putting green-brain connection into practice — Mirror–Link–Pause

Your verbal and nonverbal communication is the most powerful tool that you have to achieve green-brain connection. The easiest way of explaining this mindful communication technique is by looking at our interactions with children.

Children's emotions are big and clear to see, and because of this your response to them will be easy to identify.

Think about a young child; this can be your own child, a child you know, or an imaginary child. Picture them standing in front of you with a big smile and twinkly eyes and showing you a drawing that they made for you. As you are picturing this, notice what happens to your posture and facial expression. Do you feel a tendency to come down to their level? To raise your eyebrows, to smile and react in a way that echoes their enthusiasm? For most people, the answer will be yes. As humans, our automatic response to another person's happiness is to *mirror* their facial expressions and their posture. Because children have such strong emotions and show them in such a clear way, the effect will be even clearer than if you were talking to an adult. When you mirror the child's happiness they will feel heard, acknowledged and validated.

Then your attention is likely to move from the child to the drawing. You will look at it and ask questions about it and comment on how beautiful it is. This step is called the *link*. You are making a link between the happiness of the child and the thing that they are so happy and excited about. For example:

When you *link* the happiness to the drawing, the child feels that you really notice and appreciate what they are feeling happy about. This shows the child that you understand why they are feeling happy.

After the mirroring and linking comes the *pause*. The pause does two things. First, it allows the child's brain to really take in your response. Second, it gives the child the opportunity to initiate the next step. This prevents the child from feeling rushed or cut off. When given this time, it usually doesn't take long for the child to easily and comfortably move on to the next thing.

Mirror–Link–Pause with sadness

Now think of the same child, standing right in front of you. This time the child is crying. Tears are streaming down their face, their eyebrows are frowning and the corners of their mouth are pointing downwards. While you watch this image in your mind, do you notice a tendency to make a sad face yourself? This *mirrors* their facial expression and is the first step in the Mirror–Link–Pause process we have just discussed. A likely response to a crying child is the question, 'What happened?' Imagine the child pointing to their knee and telling you, 'I fell and hurt my knee.' You are now likely to focus on the knee, to look at it and examine how serious the fall was. By doing this you *link* the emotion to the trigger.

Often parents respond to their crying child by saying: 'You are fine, see, it's really not that bad.' This response is intended to make the child feel better but because it does not follow the Mirror–Link–Pause sequence it does not work. Just imagine that you have come home after a horrible day at work; you feel so awful that you could burst into tears, and when you reach out to your partner they simply say, 'You are fine, see, it's really not that bad.' How would you feel? What would you think? In situations like these, when your emotion is not mirrored and linked, your processing of the emotion will likely be blocked. When that happens there are only two options left: either you become stuck in the emotion or you suppress the emotion.

A young child's brain has not fully developed yet and they are not able to properly process their own emotions. When you tell them they are 'fine' when they are clearly upset, you are emotionally disconnecting from them and robbing them of the opportunity to process their emotion. Then they can only suppress the emotion or become stuck in the emotion, and the option they choose will mostly depend on their temperament and upbringing.

So, how do you help a child (or adult) who is upset to link their emotion to the trigger? You simply ask them, 'What happened?' When they explain the situation to you, you listen and then repeat it back to them, staying very close to the words they used. This is called using *clean language*. See the example on the following page.

Mirror

Link

Mirror and Pause

Move On

Some people fear that responding in this way will only make the child (or the adult) more upset. The truth is that it most often calms them down very quickly. Even if the other person does not calm down immediately, they are just letting air out of their emotional balloon, and that's a good thing! In green-brain communication the goal is not to restore calm as quickly as possible, it is to offer connection so the person's emotion can be processed without suppression, allowing the green brain to take over again. When you Mirror–Link–Pause, you are offering connection. The other person will feel heard, validated and cared for by your response, which allows their brain to process the emotion they are feeling and return to a green-brain state where they can move on from what happened. When this process is facilitated in a child, they learn how to process their own emotions using Acknowledge–Link–Let Go, which is the individual version of Mirror–Link–Pause.

Mirror–Link–Pause with anger

Again, imagine the same child standing right in front of you. This time they are frowning heavily and looking very angry. The child yells at you, 'Johnny took my toy again!' Common responses of parents include, 'Well, you can find another toy to play with,' or 'It's good to be able to share,' or 'When he is finished with it you can have it again, just play with something else in the meantime.' Now, imagine for a moment that someone comes along and just takes your phone without asking and refuses to give it back. How would you feel? What would you think? Then imagine that when you go to the authorities in order to get it back, they respond with, 'Just find something else to play with.' How would this response make you feel? To a child a toy has the same value that your phone has to you.

Because this response does not follow the Mirror–Link–Pause sequence, it does not allow for emotions to be processed. The angry child then has two options left. The first option is to become stuck in the anger. When the child becomes even angrier because the conditions to process the emotion are not facilitated, they risk being told off and emotionally rejected by their parent. See the example on the following page.

The other option the child has is to suppress the anger. Suppressed emotions lead to increased stress. In children this can lead to issues such as trouble sleeping, fears, tantrums, refusing to eat, nightmares and trouble concentrating.

To avoid this and encourage the child to process the emotion, the adult can mirror, link and then pause. See the following page for an example.

Mirror

Link and Pause

Link and Pause

Move On

Mirror–Link–Pause works well with both children and adults. You simply adjust your verbal and non-verbal language to match the age of the person you are talking to.

Here are a few examples given by course participants.

'I applied this technique to my husband when he was really upset about a leakage in the house. He said, "That's it, we're selling this house!" Usually I would have told him to just calm down and that no, we are not selling the house. This time, I applied Mirror–Link–Pause and said, "I know, it's terribly frustrating that we keep having these problems!" It felt like we were on the same team and he calmed down straightaway. After only a few minutes he no longer wanted to sell the house, and we came up with a good solution to the problem.'

'My boss often becomes stressed and then he starts to make unrealistic demands. Instead of joining him in the state of stress, I stayed calm and said, "It's so stressful when clients make all these demands." This calmed him down and we were able to discuss the issue and come up with a plan.'

'As a teacher I found this technique especially helpful with special-needs children. At school we have an autistic child who fixates on spots on her clothing. Instead of reassuring her that there are no spots on her shirt I said to her, "Those spots are really bothering you." To my surprise she then calmed down and moved on very quickly.'

The Pause in Mirror–Link–Pause

The importance of the pause is often overlooked. The pause creates space for the mirroring and the linking to have its effect on the other person's brain. This doesn't have to take longer than a few seconds, but these few seconds are important. It is hard for the brain to process something when it has to also listen to what you are saying.

Giving it a few seconds of silence allows the brain to process the emotion. Many people feel uncomfortable with a silence, but it is important to realize that the pause might be uncomfortable for you but not for the other person.

Usually the switch to green brain happens during the pause. This shift happens in the brain and the rest of the body follows. Often a change in eye gaze and posture is noticeable, accompanied by an out-breath and relaxation of the shoulders and a shift to acceptance and solution-based language. The body moves into the natural green-brain state in terms of breathing, muscle tension and vision, and the mind moves into green-brain thinking through reconnecting with the bigger picture and problem-solving. For example:

Friend: 'I haven't had a good night's sleep in weeks. Jane is driving me nuts!'

You: 'That must be exhausting.'

Friend: 'Yes, it is.'

Pause.

Friend: (sighing) 'I guess it won't be this way forever, though.'

You: 'No, it won't last forever.'

~

Partner: 'I thought you would cook tonight. You need to let me know in advance if you change your plans!'

You: 'I'm sorry. I can imagine it's frustrating for you if I change my plans and forget to tell you.'

Partner: 'Yes, it is!'

Pause.

Partner: (sighing) 'Okay, we'll just order a takeaway, but next time please let me know on time.'

Clean language

Using clean language will make the Mirror–Link–Pause technique more effective. Clean language means that you use words the other person has used or something very similar. This helps them to focus on their emotions instead of making sure you understand how they feel. For example:

No clean language

Colleague: 'I am so annoyed with Jim.'

You: 'You're angry with Jim?'

Colleague: 'Not angry, just annoyed.'

~

Clean language

Colleague: 'I am so annoyed with Jim.'

You: 'You're annoyed with Jim?'

Colleague: 'Yes, I am. He keeps changing his mind and giving me more work!'

You: 'That is annoying.'

~

No clean language

Friend: 'I really don't know what I've done wrong.'

You: 'You must feel so sad.'

Friend: 'I feel more confused, because I can't figure out what I've done wrong.'

~

Clean language

Friend: 'I really don't know what I've done wrong.'

You: 'You think you've done something wrong but you don't know what?'

Friend: 'Yes, exactly! I just can't figure it out.'

~

If the person does not tell you how they are feeling, it is fine to make assumptions based on their body language and their story. As you can see in the above examples, the other person will correct you if you get it wrong. For example:

Friend: 'Sarah is flunking school, I just got a call from her teacher.'

You: 'How upsetting.' Or 'I can imagine you feel very upset.' Or 'That must be very upsetting.'

Friend: 'Yes, it is.'

~

Client: 'I was driving and all of a sudden a car was coming at me and he was in my lane. I don't know how it got there. The next thing I knew there was a big crash.'

Therapist: 'I can imagine you were feeling very scared.' Or 'How scary.' Or 'That must have been very scary.'

Client: 'Yes, it was.'

~

Whenever you reflect back the emotion, you are encouraging the other person to focus on the emotional side of the situation. When you use clean language to reflect back the factual side of their story, you are encouraging them to elaborate on that. For example:

Focus on the facts

Colleague: 'My boss is so stressed it's driving me crazy!'

You: 'Your boss is stressed?'

Colleague: 'Yes, he runs around like a headless chicken and keeps adding things to my list that are not even my responsibility.'

~

Focus on the emotion

Colleague: 'My boss is so stressed it's driving me crazy!'

You: 'It's driving you crazy?'

Colleague: 'Yes, I'm getting really stressed too because of the way he's behaving.'

~

Focus on the facts

Client: (looking upset) 'It's been a difficult week.'

Therapist: 'A difficult week?'

Client: 'Yes, Shaun left me on Monday.'

Focus on the emotion

Client: (looking upset) 'It's been a difficult week.'

Therapist: 'You seem very upset.'

Client: 'Yes, I am. Very upset. I just don't know what to do.'

You can use both approaches in the same conversation — just remember that the other person will be inclined to elaborate on what you reflect back with clean language. When people stick to the facts rather than the emotion underlying the situation, it can be helpful to focus on the emotional side using clean language. This allows for the facts to be discussed as well as for the emotion to be processed.

How to use Mirror–Link–Pause

This technique does not replace what you would normally do, whether it be setting boundaries for a child or offering solutions or encouragement to a friend or colleague; it is an 'add on' to activate green brain in the other person so that your next step will be more effective.

'Connect before you direct.'

— *Daniel Siegel*

For example: setting boundaries.

A child has hit another child.

Mirror

Link

Link and Pause

Boundary Setting

What if Mirror–Link–Pause doesn't work?

When you apply this technique to people who are very close to you and have known you for a long time, there is a chance they will respond to the change in your approach rather than the technique. They may even feel like you are making fun of them. To avoid this, it is important to start by making small changes to your interactions. You can see your way of communicating with them as a dance: you have been dancing the same dance for years, and if you change the steps all of a sudden it can be confusing and may even feel unsafe for the other person. Their initial response will be to pull you back into the familiar routine. If you can make the changes subtle enough, you can change the dance into a better one without triggering resistance. Also remember that changing patterns is not easy; it comes with practice and it comes with time. If the technique doesn't work all at once, don't give up; evaluate and try again. Simply listening to them and not responding by saying anything that starts with *At least* ... is a good way to start improving green-brain connection.

What if the person becomes more upset?

If a person — adult or child — becomes more emotional when you apply the Mirror–Link–Pause technique it is probably because you are creating space for their emotions, which invites them to blow off steam. Remember that this is a healthy and necessary step to processing emotions. When someone becomes overwhelmed you can pause and just give them a big hug, or you can calm them down by having them focus on something else and then come back to the topic at a later time.

What if another emotion comes up?

We all have different layers of emotions. Frustration and anger often show up first. When you use the Mirror–Link–Pause technique you can help someone process the first layer of emotion; after that, the underlying emotion will come up. Often this is sadness or fear. When this happens, just follow the steps again. When you can notice physical relaxation and the move to acceptance and problem-solving language, you know that the emotions have been processed.

Integrate

The way I have described the technique is very black-and-white. In real life you will naturally mix the technique up with your own way of communicating. The idea is to practise the technique and then integrate it into your communication in a way that works well for you. In time you will notice that you leave more space for other people's emotions and stop trying to fix them or make them feel better by distracting them with

At least... You will notice that green brain connection happens when you can accept their uncomfortable emotions and be understanding and non-judgmental about them. Offering the reassurance that the way they are feeling makes perfect sense in the situation is more powerful than offering solutions. You are respectfully facilitating the processing of their own emotions, without cutting the process short. When you allow this to happen you will witness the way people visibly shift from the red- to the green-brain state and start to come up with great solutions themselves — solutions that you could have never thought of.

INSIGHT INSPIRATION

1. When someone around you is feeling a negative emotion, how do you usually respond? Do you tell them *At least*...? Do you give advice? Do you try to come up with solutions or suggestions?

_____

_____

2. With whom would you like to have more mindful connection?

_____

_____

3. As an experiment observe how you respond to their emotions and try the MLP technique for a week. What have you noticed?

_____

_____

_____

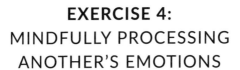

EXERCISE 4:
MINDFULLY PROCESSING ANOTHER'S EMOTIONS

Mirror

STEP 1. Mirror the facial expression and body posture of the other person.

STEP 2. Acknowledge their emotion. For example:

> » How upsetting/annoying/stressful/sad/etc.
> » I can see that you feel very upset/annoyed/stressed/sad/etc.
> » You must be feeling upset/annoyed/stressed/sad/etc.

Link

STEP 3. Link the emotion to the trigger. For example:

> » What happened?
> » Tell me more.

STEP 4. Use clean language to mention the trigger as they described it.

Pause

STEP 5. Pause for a few seconds.

If the person still seems emotional: repeat steps **1 to 5.**
If another emotion comes up: repeat steps **1 to 5.**
If they stay on a factual level: focus on mirroring the emotion.

Once you see the change in eye gaze, posture and language to acceptance and problem-solving language, the emotion has been processed.

RENEW YOUR MIND TIP

Use 'clean language' in everyday situations, even when the person you are speaking with is not upset. It will improve the connection because it makes them feel like you really get what they are saying.

CHAPTER 5:

The power of thoughts

The way you navigate through life largely depends on your thoughts. They determine how you feel and influence your decisions and your actions — every part of your life that you can control. Your thinking is one of the most powerful tools you will ever have in changing your life and creating happiness. Let me explain why.

The key to happiness is not a perfect life and if it was that would be very, very sad because none of us has a perfect life. Yes, some of us suffer way more than others, but as anyone who has travelled and visited Third World countries or remote villages will tell you, often the people who supposedly have 'nothing' are so happy! They might live in a hut, have no running water and no electricity, but they seem to be so much happier than most people in the West who have all of these things and so much more. So, the good news is that happiness does not depend on your circumstances. You can stop trying to create the perfect life to achieve a state of happiness;

it simply won't work because it is not how happiness is created. What creates happiness is your thoughts. Or, to put it differently, our natural state is happiness but our thoughts rob us of our happiness. Training your thoughts to simply stop doing this to you is therefore the way to a happier life. In order to be happy you need to renew your mind and train your brain to replace your bad thinking habits that rob you of your happiness with thinking habits that make you happier regardless of the circumstances.

The Cognitive Behavioural Therapy (CBT) model is one of the most important models in psychology. This model states that events lead to thoughts, thoughts lead to feelings, feelings to behaviours, and behaviours have consequences. It is not the events themselves that determine how you feel and behave; *it is the thoughts you have about these events* that trigger the sequence of feelings, behaviours and consequences. As with every model, it is a simplification of a complex and dynamic reality. However, it is a very useful tool that gives insight into how the mind works and how we can make it work better.

Cognitive Behavioural Therapy model

Here are some examples of the CBT model.

Example 1

Scenario 1

Event	You are standing on a stage, about to give a presentation. You look out into the room and see a large group of people. Your heart begins to beat faster and your hands become sweaty.
Thought	Then you think, 'Oh no, what a large group. I can't do this!'
Feelings	You feel anxious, nervous and insecure.
Behaviour	You forget the words, make mistakes and speak too quickly.
Consequence	Your performance is less than it could have been and you feel bad about it afterwards.

Scenario 2

Event	You are standing on a stage, about to give a presentation. You look out into the room and see a large group of people. Your heart begins to beat faster and your hands become sweaty.
Thought	Then you think, 'Oh wow, what a large group. This is going to be great!'
Feelings	You feel energized, confident and excited.
Behaviour	You speak with confidence and remember your text, and your enthusiasm is noticeable.
Consequence	Your performance is great and you feel happy and satisfied afterwards.

The event is the same, but different thoughts about the event lead to completely different outcomes. In the first scenario you perceive the event as threatening, activating the red brain, which makes it hard to perform well. In the second scenario your thoughts are non-threatening, activating the orange or green brain, which support good performance.

Another example. Let's say you are lying in bed and you suddenly hear a loud bang. This is an event. If you then think to yourself 'It is a burglar' you will probably feel scared. Your personality and past experiences will determine your actions, but let's say you 'freeze'. You feel scared and hide under the blankets — a likely consequence of this is that it will take a long time for you to fall asleep and you will feel tired the next day.

Example 2

Scenario 1

Event	You are lying in bed and you hear a loud bang.
Thought	Then you think, 'It's a burglar!'
Feelings	You feel scared and vulnerable.
Behaviour	You freeze and hide under the blankets.
Consequence	You lie awake for hours, and after eventually falling into a restless sleep you feel tired and cranky the next day.

Scenario 2

Event	You are lying in bed and you hear a loud bang.
Thought	Then you think, 'It's just the neighbour's cat.'
Feelings	You feel relieved.
Behaviour	You relax and fall asleep.
Consequence	You get a good night's sleep and wake up the following morning feeling rested.

Again, the exact same event can have two completely different outcomes. The outcome does not depend on the event but on your thoughts about the event. In the first scenario the red brain is activated because your mind perceives a threat when thinking the sound is made by a burglar. This perceived threat activates the stress response and in this situation the triggered emotion is fear. In the second scenario, the same event has a very different outcome. The thought about the event is a non-threatening, non-judgmental one, therefore it activates the green brain. This leads to feeling relieved, relaxed and having a good night's sleep.

These examples show that it is your interpretation (i.e. what you think is going on) that activates either the green or the red brain. This is important because often you cannot change your situation or circumstances but you are able to change your thoughts and therefore create a very different outcome, even if the situation remains unchanged. The only exception to this would be if the situation is a real emergency. Then your system automatically activates red brain as it is the appropriate brain state to deal with an emergency

Science

An eight-year study by the University of Wisconsin–Madison shows that if you have been under a lot of stress in the past 12 months the risk of premature death increases by 43 per cent.

One of the most interesting findings is that this was found to be true only for the people who also *believed* that stress was harmful to their health. People who experienced significant stress but did not see stress as harmful were no more likely to die prematurely. In fact, they had the lowest risk of premature death, even lower than the people in the study who experienced little stress! When you view stress symptoms such as increased heart rate, breathing and that adrenaline rush as positive signs that your body is getting ready to meet a challenge, there seems to be no negative effect on your health.

In a study conducted by Harvard University, researchers told participants with induced stress to view their increased heart rate as a sign their body was getting ready to perform, and their change in breathing as a helpful response because the body was pumping more oxygen to the brain. When participants started to see these stress symptoms as helpful they became less stressed and anxious and more confident. When participants viewed their stress symptoms as positive their heart rate increased but their blood vessels did not become narrow (a combination associated with a normal stress response); instead, the vessels stayed relaxed. This state of increased heart rate combined with relaxed blood vessels resembles the body's response in moments of joy and courage. In the usual stress response, increased heart rate combined with narrowed blood vessels leads to an unhealthy state that increases the risk of cardiovascular disease.

These studies and others like it tell us that when you change your mind about stress, you can change your physical response to stress. If you control your thoughts and keep them neutral or positive, you can use the stress response and turn it into a moment of joy and confidence rather than a moment of anxiety and stress. Over time this could mean the difference between a stress-induced heart attack leading to premature death or living a long and healthy life.

Core beliefs

Your thoughts, whether you are in green, orange or red brain, are part of your conscious mind. But they don't stand on their own. They are a result of what is happening in your subconscious mind. Your subconscious mind contains many different things including memories, feelings and thoughts, and at the very 'bottom' of your subconscious mind are what we call the core beliefs. Your red brain thoughts are connected to your red-brain core beliefs, feelings and drive. Red brain is activated when your thoughts about circumstances or things make you feel physically or emotionally unsafe or not in control. Your orange brain thoughts are connected to core beliefs centred around what you think you have to do in order to stay okay or in control. Orange brain tells you that your 'okayness' or safety depends on your ability to *do* certain things. Green brain thoughts, however, are linked to green-brain core beliefs of being okay and safe *as you are*. These subconscious thoughts and core beliefs are established in early childhood and are the fundamental building blocks of your thoughts and, therefore, your happiness.

	RED BRAIN	ORANGE BRAIN	GREEN BRAIN
Conscious thoughts	Fighting reality	I have to .../ You need to ...	Observant, non-judgmental, acceptance of situations and boundaries
Feelings	Unhappy: sad, anxious or frustrated/angry	Conditional happiness as long as the 'have tos and need tos' are met	Base feeling = happy Allows for processing of sadness, fear, anger
Drive	Fighting reality: complaining, blaming, panicking, forcing	Having to keep going: performing/ controlling/pleasing/ staying strong/staying dependent/fixing (fulfilling the set conditions to be okay)	Curiosity, interest, motivation, enjoyment, values-based action, responds to situations with acceptance or 'what would help?'
Sub-conscious thoughts	Things are not okay	For things to be okay I need to .../you need to ...	Everything is okay
Core beliefs	I am not okay/ I am bad I am rejected I am unsafe	I am not good enough I am only okay as long as ... I am only accepted as long as ... I am safe as long as ...	I am okay I am accepted I am safe

Because your core beliefs are part of your subconscious mind, they are not always readily available for introspection. They are like glasses through which you see the world and the events that happen in your life — the only issue is, most people don't know they are wearing these glasses. Therefore, your belief about the world *is* as you *see* the world, not realizing it might be your dark or rose-tinted glasses colouring what you see. Naturally, therefore, you project your core beliefs about yourself and the world onto everything you see and believe that you are seeing things clearly and accurately. This is reinforced because your core beliefs *feel* so strong and so true.

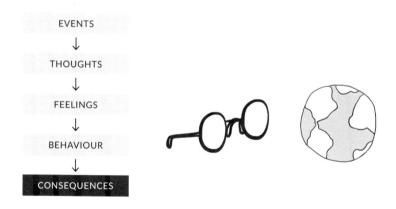

EVENTS
↓
THOUGHTS
↓
FEELINGS
↓
BEHAVIOUR
↓
CONSEQUENCES

For example, one client had the core belief that she was not good enough and that no one liked her. As soon as she walked into a room full of people she would convince herself that no one there liked her and that they did not want her to be there. She was projecting her thoughts and feelings onto the people in the room, looking through her glasses and believing that what she saw were the thoughts and feelings of these other people. This feeling was so strong and felt so true that she never questioned it; she just accepted it as the truth.

In time a core belief can become a self-fulfilling prophecy; something that becomes true not because it was originally true but as a consequence of how people respond to your behaviour. In this example, my client became insecure and withdrawn when she was around other people. This stopped her from being her usual fun and loving self. Instead she would be quiet and try to find an excuse to leave as soon as possible. Because of this behaviour, in time people started to think that *she* did not like *them* very much and that she did not want to be there. They probably started to see her as withdrawn, cold and not very much fun to be around, which led to her not being invited to events. In this way, her core belief came full circle and actually turned into the reality.

It's such a dark place out there.

It's such a happy place out there.

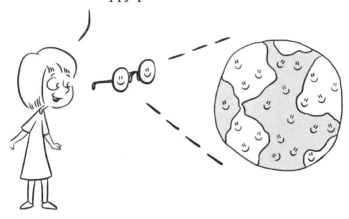

Another example is a client who had a core belief that the world is a dangerous place. This made him constantly on edge and vigilant (overactive red brain), and his mind was constantly looking for evidence that he was right. He planned his every action by calculating risks. To him this way of living made perfect sense, because the belief *felt* so true and rational. However, he did suffer from chronic stress, digestive issues, relationship difficulties and had trouble sleeping. These were likely a result of his overactive red brain and chronic high stress. In time this could turn into a self-fulfilling prophecy: because of his high stress level and lack of sleep he might be unable to focus well or see the bigger picture, which would make him more prone to making mistakes. This could then lead to dangerous situations.

'Thoughts become things.'

— *Unknown*

The origin of core beliefs

Core beliefs are formed early on in life, and they are a result of the emotional environment you grew up in. Significant life events and your personality also play a big role in shaping your core beliefs.

Because core beliefs are formed when you are still a young child, they are formed with a child's brain and therefore depict child-like thinking, which can be characterized as self-centred, and black-and-white, all-or-nothing thinking. Core beliefs are self-centred because this is the way children see the world. A child always believes it is 'all about them'. When their parent is angry they don't have the brain capacity yet to see the bigger picture and think 'Mum is just having a bad day today because of the pressures at work. This is not because of me.' Instead they will automatically assume it is because of them.

Core beliefs can be positive, neutral or negative. Examples of positive core beliefs are *I am okay, I am loved* or *I am smart*. A common negative core belief is *I am not good enough*. This is a very judgmental and black-and-white thought that leaves no room for nuance; it focuses completely on the person

123

holding the core belief. It is unspecific and therefore can be applied to any situation. It is a common core belief for people who grew up with conditional love or unpredictable love and acceptance.

Other common core beliefs are *I am bad* or *It is my fault*. Again, these thoughts are very black-and-white, all-or-nothing, self-centred and unspecific. These or similar core beliefs are common for people who grew up with an abusive, dismissive or emotionally unavailable parent. Because children completely depend on their parents or caregivers for food, shelter and emotional care, children are incredibly loyal to their parents or caregivers. Emotionally rejecting the parent would endanger their chances of survival, so a child's brain is programmed to stay emotionally loyal to the parent no matter what. The only way to stay loyal to a dismissive, abusive or (emotionally) neglectful parent is to believe that you deserve to be treated this way and side *with* the parent. This is how the core belief *I am bad* or *I am not good enough* is founded.

One client had a powerful insight during a green-brain exercise in our session. In her mind, she was taken back to a situation that happened when she was only eight years old when her father had touched her inappropriately. After the event she was in the kitchen with her family, sitting around the kitchen table, when she mentioned what had happened. Then her father looked at her in disgust with both fear and anger showing on his face. Because she was only a child she had no choice but to stay emotionally loyal to her father, because it would render her unsafe to lose the 'acceptance' of the adult on whom she was completely dependent. Therefore, in that moment, her negative thoughts and feelings about her father flipped around and became directed at herself. She decided that there must be something wrong with *her*; she started to believe that she was disgusting and bad. She agreed with the adult because to a young child's brain, disagreeing is even more unsafe. The sad consequence is that in that moment, when her core beliefs *I am bad* and *There is something wrong with me* were born, her internal world became unsafe.

The link

When a home situation is filled with negative dynamics and emotions, a child will pick up on them. This aligns with step 1 of the Acknowledge–Link–Let Go (ALL) theory of processing emotions. The child might not be able to consciously acknowledge and name the emotions, but on a subconscious level they pick up on tension very quickly (step 1: Acknowledge). The child's brain will then automatically look for the link (step 2: Link). The correct response would be to link the negative emotion to the parent — after all, it is the parent who is responsible for these negative dynamics; the child is just a child and can never be held responsible.

But because in a child's brain the world revolves around them and it is dangerous to be emotionally disloyal to their parents, they are more likely to link the negative emotion to themselves. So, when you yell or scream or argue with your partner in the presence of your child, the child will pick up on the negative emotion (step 1: Acknowledge), and because of the way their brain works, they are likely to link it to themselves (step 2: Link). The child will see themselves as the cause of the negative emotion and when this is an ongoing dynamic, core beliefs such as *I am bad* or *It is my fault* are created.

For example, one of my clients has two sons: an adult son and a little boy who was aged three at the time. The eldest son had drug issues and was in trouble with the law. Understandably this led to anger and tension in the house. The three-year-old boy picked up on these negative dynamics, and within the course of a week he went from being a happy and content young boy (green-brain state) to a sad, withdrawn child. He started to say things like, 'I am useless' and 'Everyone is angry with me' (red-brain state). Of course this upset the parents and they tried to explain that they were not angry with him but they did not want to burden him with the knowledge of what was going on with his brother. They told him that everything was fine and they were not angry with him. This was not effective, because everything was not fine, and denying the tension or even acknowledging it without offering a link did not relieve the child from linking the emotions to himself.

After the mother learned the ALL technique, they changed their approach from telling the child that everything was fine (which it was not) to acknowledging that 'Yes, Mummy and Daddy are really angry' (step 1. Acknowledge). Then they offered a link that was understandable to a three-year-old by pointing out that his older brother had parked his car on the grass, leaving marks. They said, 'We are really angry with your brother because he parked his car on the grass and cars belong on the road. Look, the lawn is very damaged!' The mother described how in that moment her son became silent and thought deeply for a few seconds. She could see the 'aha moment' on his face when he dropped his shoulders and he said, 'Yes, Mummy, it was very naughty of him to park his car on the grass, cars belong on the road not on the grass!' After that he went back to being his normal self. He was now able to link the negative emotions to something the older brother had done (linking to an action is always better than linking to a person) and therefore he could understand, process and let go. In this example we gain a rare insight into a three-year-old's way of thinking and how children link negative emotions to themselves when there is no clear trigger to link them to.

When parents say things like, 'You are so slow,' 'What's wrong with you?' or 'I am not happy with you,' they offer links the child remembers and continues to use in their self-talk even into adulthood. The way your parents made you feel either by what they said or what they did becomes part of your subconscious thoughts and core beliefs, and these in turn shape your conscious thoughts and your internal dialogue — your self-talk. In psychology this part is often referred to as the internal critical parent. The internal critical parent is a part of the adult that continues the trend the parents have started. I believe that this process is at the core of why so many people are unduly hard on themselves.

Why are core beliefs important?

Gaining insight into your core beliefs and understanding their origins helps you to identify and understand the glasses you are wearing. This insight allows your mind to open up to the possibility that things might not *be* true even when they *feel* true. Something is not true just because it feels true; it could be your glasses, your projections, your subconscious core beliefs that you are seeing rather than reality.

The Acknowledge–Link–Let Go (ALL) process helps you to become aware of your glasses and to see the world around you more objectively. Once you understand your core beliefs they can provide a powerful link in the ALL process. When you have insight into your most important links and accept that your emotions make perfect sense given what you have gone through, it is a lot easier to let go of them. As you continue to practise the ALL technique, your core beliefs and self-talk become less rigid, which gives you greater awareness and control of your feelings. Your internal world becomes safer and you can move from beating yourself up to backing yourself up.

Here are some examples of how ALL links with core beliefs.

~

Hello feeling like nobody likes me.

It makes perfect sense that you are here because I grew up feeling like a burden to my parents.

Take a deep breath, drop your shoulders and let it go.

~

Hello feeling anxious.

It makes perfect sense that you are here because when I was a child my father was very anxious and always told me the world is a dangerous place and I believed him.

Take a deep breath, drop your shoulders and let it go.

~

Hello feeling bad about myself.

It makes perfect sense that you are here because when I spoke about what Dad had done he turned on me and looked at me in disgust. I had no choice but to agree with him and see myself as disgusting and bad. It makes perfect sense that I feel this way but it does not make it true.

Take a deep breath, drop your shoulders and let it go.

Training green brain through thoughts

As soon as you feel judged by someone else or by your own negative self-talk, the automatic response is for the brain to move towards the red zone. Judging yourself with negative self-talk coming from negative core beliefs is therefore a powerful red-brain trigger. Mindfulness trains your mind to see clearly and not get caught up in believing your projections. It reshapes your internal dialogue and self-talk, which leads to increased self-compassion. Then the critical inner voice can begin to be dismantled and a more mindful, kind and caring voice can start to develop.

There are several ways you can train your mind to have fewer and fewer thoughts that trigger red brain and more thoughts that promote green brain and protect your happiness. An important step is to put a new filter on your inner dialogue. The first step in doing this is to become more aware of your thoughts and understand that they make perfect sense but are not necessarily true or useful or even acceptable according to your own standards. Imagine your thoughts being broadcast out loud. What would that be like? Or take a moment to think about some of the things you say to yourself on a regular basis when you are stressed or under pressure. Now say these things out loud, pretending you are talking to a friend. What do your thoughts sound like now? If your self-talk is anything like my self-talk was before I started training my thoughts, your thoughts are negative, harsh, critical and untrue. It's likely that you sound like a real bully when you speak out loud the self-talk that is so normal to you in the privacy of your own mind. The truth is that many people are self-bullying all the time but you wouldn't have a clue based on their outward appearance. The first step to changing this is increased awareness of the thoughts and how unhelpful they are.

The second step is to begin to filter out the unhelpful thoughts. One way to do this is to make a conscious decision to only give radio time to joyful or helpful thoughts and kindly silence the stressful and unhelpful thoughts. Yes, this is hard but it can be done. You don't accept that kind of language from others, so don't accept it from yourself either. Simply tell your mind to stop it and replace it with a joyful or helpful thought. It might feel impossible in the beginning but if you stick to it after only a week of resisting unhelpful thoughts and replacing them with helpful thoughts, you will think and feel very differently.

For example, the thought *My family is on the other side of the world* is a thought that only brings me sadness, and it is a useless thought because it doesn't make my family move closer to me. *My family is only a plane ride away* is much more helpful.

The thought *I need to get this done* triggers stress. *I would like to get this done and will do my very best to finish it on time but if I can't I will find a solution* is much more helpful.

The thought *I have lost an important client* brings negative emotions plus it is a useless thought because it doesn't bring the client back. *There will be plenty of other opportunities* is much more helpful.

The thought *I am exhausted* only makes me feel more tired. The thought *I will make it through the day and get an early night* is much more helpful.

Another way to start retraining your thoughts is by consciously erasing the shoulds and shouldn'ts from your thinking. Simply decide that these words are no longer allowed.

I shouldn't waste my time becomes *I will spend my time on things I love.*

She shouldn't be so stupid becomes *She can think and do what she wants but I'm no longer investing energy in this relationship.*

The neighbours should be more considerate becomes *It is what it is, let's have a friendly chat about the volume of the music.*

Many clients and course participants see changing their self-talk as the greatest benefit of learning to renew their mind. When you become more compassionate, kinder and less judgmental towards yourself, your internal world becomes a safer place and you will spend more and more time in green brain as a result. This leads to you feeling calmer, happier and more in control. Because of this, changing your thoughts can soften and, in time, undo the internal patterns that were created in a negative childhood dynamic.

There will always be events and circumstances in your life that you cannot control. But if you learn to control your thoughts, suddenly your mood and behaviour no longer depend on your circumstances but on you.

INSIGHT INSPIRATION

1. Write down your three most often occurring stressful thoughts — three thoughts that you have on a regular basis that make you feel stressed. For example, *I don't have enough money. I am not a good mother. I don't have enough time. I hate my job.*

   _____

   _____

   _____

2. Finish these sentences with the very first thing that comes to your mind, even if it does not make any sense.

   I am _____

   Others are _____

   I have to be _____ or else _____

   _____

   The world is _____

3. As a child what was your role in the family? For example, *the rebel, the smart one, the helper, the peacemaker, the golden child, the parent, the baby, the difficult one.*

   _____

4. Take a moment to look at your answers to the above questions. Are your recurring stressful thoughts and your answers to question 2 linked? And how do your stressful thoughts relate to your role in the family as a child?

   _____

   _____

5. How have these thoughts and beliefs impacted your life?

_____

_____

_____

_____

6. Look at your stressful thoughts and identify which emotion they bring out in you. Then look at your beliefs about yourself and the world (question 2) and your role in the family as a child. Why does this emotion make perfect sense? Use these insights for the ALL process and practise these on a regular basis.

_____

_____

_____

_____

_____

ALL for stressful thought 1.

STEP 1. Hello _____ (emotion)

STEP 2. It makes perfect sense that you are here because

_____

_____

STEP 3. Breathe out, drop your shoulders and let it go.

--- ≋ ---

ALL for stressful thought 2.

STEP 1. Hello _____ (emotion)

STEP 2. It makes perfect sense that you are here because

_____

_____

STEP 3. Breathe out, drop your shoulders and let it go.

~

ALL for stressful thought 3.

STEP 1. Hello _____ (emotion)

STEP 2. It makes perfect sense that you are here because

_____

_____

STEP 3. Breathe out, drop your shoulders and let it go.

CHAPTER 6:

Renew your mind, change your thoughts

When you begin to renew your mind and train your brain, you will recognize your recurring stressful thoughts and become more aware of how quickly they make your red brain kick into gear. The next logical question is: how do I change my stressful thoughts?

General mindfulness practice retrains your brain, and it retrains your thinking to be kinder and less judgmental. This will lead to an overall reduction of stressful thoughts. However, we each have deeply rooted specific stressful thoughts that are hard to get rid of. It can be very useful, besides your regular mindfulness practice, to pay some extra attention to these thoughts and work on changing them into more helpful thoughts. There are several ways in which you can do this. In my experience, the self-enquiry technique by Byron Katie is one of the most effective ways of changing persistent, stressful or negative thoughts.

Byron Katie's approach has deeply impacted my 'thought life'. In her book *Loving What Is*, she describes how in 1986, at the bottom of a ten-year spiral into depression, rage and self-loathing, she woke up one morning to a state of constant joy that has never left her. She realized that when she believed her stressful thoughts, she suffered, but that when she questioned them, she didn't suffer, and that this is true for every human being. Her simple yet powerful process of enquiry is called The Work (www.thework.com).

Byron Katie's self-enquiry technique gently forces you to take a step back and look at your stressful thoughts from a different perspective. Then you cannot help but start seeing things differently. When you become unstuck from your stressful thoughts, you find out that they are indeed just thoughts. Thoughts that make perfect sense given what you have gone through. Thoughts that feel very true but are not necessarily true.

Identifying your stressful thoughts

According to the CBT model, an event that triggers a stressful thought leads to feelings of stress and a red-brain reaction, which often has negative consequences. In order to change this sequence you first need to identify the thought that is triggering the stress. It is not always easy to identify your thoughts, but you can recognize when you are becoming stressed. You may notice your shoulders becoming tense, your breathing becoming shallow and your heart starting to beat faster. Most people describe it as a feeling of pressure and restriction on their chest, in their head or stomach. One way of identifying your stressful thoughts is to pause when you have these feelings and focus on your thoughts in that moment. Another way to identify your stressful thoughts is to think about a situation that makes you feel stressed or an unpleasant emotion, then bring your awareness to your thoughts.

Your thoughts consist of many layers. The top layers are often nicely constructed and are a lot more reasonable than the lower layers. The closer to the underlying, raw and 'ugly' thought, the more effect the technique will have. Here is an example:

Top-layer thought: *I am not sure if I can retire comfortably.*

No one can be really sure of this but it won't be stressful for everyone. This means that the stress will come from an underlying thought or fear, which could be:

I need to be sure I can retire comfortably, or

I won't be able to retire comfortably.

You can go one layer deeper by asking yourself, 'And what would happen then? What am I really afraid of?' For example:

If I can't retire comfortably, I will end up alone.

If I can't retire comfortably, I will end up homeless.

If I can't retire comfortably, I will become unhappy.

Another useful question to ask yourself is: 'If I can't retire comfortably, what would that say about me?' For example:

If I can't retire comfortably, it means that I have failed.

If I can't retire comfortably, it means I will become a burden to others and they will resent me for it.

One way to determine whether a particular thought is appropriate to use for the self-enquiry technique is to note your immediate physical response when you think or say the thought out loud. If you get an immediate unpleasant emotional or physical response you have likely found a core stressful thought. When you have identified a thought that causes you stress you can apply the following steps of Byron Katie's self-enquiry process.

Ask the questions

1. Is it true?

This first question can only be answered with a 'yes' or 'no'; 'maybe' and complicated explanations are not allowed. When you ask yourself the question, you will immediately look at your thought in a more rational way and you will find that very often the answer is *No, that thought is actually not true.* When you realize this, your perspective changes and you begin to become unstuck from the stressful thought. Other times the answer will be *Yes, that thought is true.* Regardless of whether your stressful thought is true or not, you simply answer the question and then move on to the next question.

2. Can I be absolutely sure it is true?

Again, this question can only be answered with a 'yes' or a 'no'. Often you will find that the answer is no because most of the time you cannot be 100 per cent sure that something is true or will happen. When your answer is no, the awareness comes that this thought that *feels* so true actually is not true. This creates space for further enquiry. Other times the answer may be *Yes, I can absolutely know that this thought is true.* Regardless of whether the answer is yes or no, you simply answer the question and then move on to the next question.

3. How do I react, what happens, when I believe that thought?

You can comment on how believing this thought makes you feel, how it makes you want to react and how that affects your health, happiness and relationships or perhaps work performance. For example:

When I believe the thought, 'I will lose my job if I don't perform better,' it makes me feel stressed and worried, which makes it even harder to do my job well.

When I believe the thought, 'I am ugly', I become filled with self-hatred. I then respond by binge eating and feel guilty afterwards.

Regardless of your response, by answering this question you will probably find that believing your stressful thoughts makes you feel bad and respond in ways you don't like and that aren't helpful. If you have a positive response to this question, then there is no need to use the self-enquiry process on that thought. Most people are only motivated to change thoughts that don't work for them. Feel free to keep the ones that work for you.

4. Who would I be without the thought?

If tomorrow morning you wake up and the thought is gone, completely erased from your mind, what would be different about you? What would be different about the way you feel and react and how would that change your situation? Often people respond to this question by saying, 'I would be so much lighter and more relaxed,' or 'I would be less worried and better able to do my job,' or 'I would actually enjoy my job and my life a lot more'. Whatever your answer is, envision it and let it sink in.

Turn it around

The last and perhaps most important step is the turn-around. I encourage you to see it as a thought experiment, a way to try out different thoughts to see how they work for you.

A statement can be turned around to the self, to the other, and to the opposite. For example, *Mike should understand me turns* around to:

- » Mike shouldn't understand me. (to the opposite)
- » I should understand me. (to the self)
- » I should understand Mike. (to the other)

I don't ever want to experience an argument with Mike again turns around to:

» I am willing to experience an argument with Mike again.

» I look forward to experiencing an argument with Mike again.

After you have come up with a turn-around, you then come up with at least three examples of why that turn-around is true. It is these examples that really shift your perspective and give you insights. The examples you come up with are the pieces of evidence that your brain needs to truly become unstuck from the stressful thought and begin to believe and strengthen more helpful thoughts.

For example, *Mike should understand me* turns around to:

» *Mike does not have to understand me.*

Example of why that is true: No one *has* to understand me. Whether someone does or doesn't is up to them. I cannot make him understand me just because I would like him to understand me. He does not *have* to do anything.

Practising the self-enquiry technique will teach you that no one *has* to do anything. What they do or don't do is their business, not yours. It is very stressful to believe that people should do things they are not doing; plus you believing they should doesn't actually change anything about what they do or don't do. When you believe someone *has* to do something, you are interfering with their personal responsibility, when actually the only thing you can control is what *you* do. Therefore, it is a way of thinking that could easily lead to stress. Of course, you would prefer it if people did things a certain way, but that is not the same thing as believing they *should* do things a certain way.

The release that comes from realizing that other people don't have to do anything and you can control only your own life gives so much freedom. This does not mean that you no longer share with others your opinion or requests, but you leave with them the responsibility of what they do with that. It is their business; what you do and how you respond to them is your business. Even when the person you are talking to is your partner or grown-up child, ultimately they are responsible for their actions. This opens up the way to genuine conversation and enquiry of their reasons behind what they do.

> *'The what-ifs and should-haves*
> *will eat your brain.'*
>
> — *John O'Callaghan*

Mike should understand me turns around to *I should understand me.*

Here is an example of why this is true.

I am so focused on Mike's behaviour that I lose sight of understanding my own thoughts and feelings. It makes me clingy, demanding and emotional, which makes him want to pull away even more. If I don't understand myself and know what it really is that I want, how can Mike understand me?

Mike should understand me turns around to *I should understand Mike.*

Here is an example of why this is true.

I have been so focused on him not understanding me that I haven't taken the time to try to understand him. Now that I think of it, I haven't been very good at listening to him or trying to give him what he needs yet I expect that he does that for me, which is not fair.

I don't ever want to experience an argument with Mike again turns around to *I am willing to experience an argument with Mike again.*

Here is an example of why this is true.

Experiencing another argument with Mike will allow me to practise my new techniques. It might be hard but it will only make me stronger and teach me valuable lessons.

I don't ever want to experience an argument with Mike again turns around to *I look forward to experiencing an argument with Mike again.*

Here is an example of why this could be true.

Experiencing another argument with Mike will only make me stronger and teach me valuable lessons. It helps us to see where things are going wrong and what we should change to make it better. Arguments are not fun but in the end we always work through them and it brings us closer together.

I have used this technique many times and it has truly reshaped some of my persistent, negative and stressful thoughts. One of my most stressful thoughts used to be, *I don't have enough time.* I used to have this thought several times a day, and every time I would feel stressed and irritated. My shoulders would become tense, my breathing would become shallow, and my heart rate would increase. The red brain would be activated swiftly and lead to tunnel vision and losing sight of the bigger picture.

My thinking became black-and-white and judgmental. This led to irritation towards the people around me, but mostly with myself. Then I started to apply the self-enquiry technique to this stressful thought: *I cannot be late.*

1. Is it true?

I cannot be late — is that true? The answer is no, because it is possible that I can be late.

2. Can I absolutely know that it is true?

No, I can't.

3. How do I react, what happens, when I believe that thought?

I feel stressed, tense and irritated. It makes me angry with myself and others. It makes me disorganized and forgetful and it creates more negative thoughts.

4. Who would I be without the thought?

Without the thought I would be much more relaxed and more patient with myself. I would probably find it easier to get more organized and plan my mornings differently so I won't be as late the next time!

5. Turn the thought around:

I *can* be late.

Why is that true?

It is a fact that I can be late. I don't like being late, but it is possible and it won't be the end of the world. In fact, probably no one at work will notice and if they do it really doesn't matter. I have been late before and it has never been an issue; I just make up the time by working longer. Wow, it is really not such a big deal at all!

Even though this exercise helped me to stress less about being late it did not have the eye-opening and calming effect I knew was possible. So, I looked at the situation again and tried to use Acknowledge–Link–Let Go in the moments I felt stressed. This made me aware of the following underlying thoughts:

» I don't have enough time.

» I am not supported.

» I might fail to do what is expected of me.

Then I thought about my role in the family as a child and replied to these thoughts by saying, *It makes perfect sense I am here, given what I have gone through.* I became aware that growing up I experienced my family and environment as one where there was never enough. There was not enough money, there was not enough time, not enough resources. I am the oldest child, I needed to be responsible and always do my best at everything. Looking back, I realized that I experienced this as having the burden of expectation and responsibility combined with a lack of resources and support. So, my thoughts made perfect sense! And they felt so true because they were my true experience when I was a child.

Doing the self-enquiry technique again, with these insights, made it easier for me to start with the right thoughts, the thoughts that were really causing the stress: *I don't have enough time.*

1. Is it true?

I don't have enough time — is that true? My first response in the moment is 'yes' it is true.

2. Can I absolutely know that it is true?

No, I can't. Because what is enough time?

3. How do I react, what happens, when I think that thought?

I feel stressed, tensed and irritated. I become frustrated with myself and it makes me disorganized and forgetful, which leads to more negative thoughts.

4. Who would I be without the thought?

Without the thought I would be more relaxed and more compassionate towards myself. This would make my mornings enjoyable and fun and I would probably find it easier to be organized and plan my mornings differently.

5. Turn the thought around:

I *do* have enough time. Actually, I have plenty of time!

Why is that true?

I have plenty of time because each of my days has 24 hours. If I arrive an hour late at work I will not have lost that hour, I will just have used it for something else. Even if I sleep in I haven't lost that time, I have used it to sleep. I can never lose time when I stay in the green-brain state, because in this state I am aware, present, kind and connected. No catastrophe will happen if some things take more time, it will be fine. I can manage it.

Here is an example of another turn-around:

Time does not have enough me.

Why is that true?

When I am stressed, irritated and impatient I am not aware, present and connected. I am unmindful and then it is true that my time does not have enough me. Every time I'm in the red-brain state the best part of me checks out and then my time does not have enough me.

This is when I got the wow, that is really true, moment. I only lose resources when I go into the red brain. Not because I am losing time but because I 'lose' the green-brain version of myself! This makes perfect sense!

The second underlying thought I had discovered was: *I am not supported.* Using the self-enquiry technique on this one was even more profound.

1. Is it true?

I am not supported — is that true? Even in the moment I can realize that no, that is not true.

2. Can I absolutely know that it is true?

No, I can't.

3. How do I react, what happens, when I think that thought?

When I believe the thought *I am not supported* I feel overburdened, anxious, lonely and disconnected. I turn into a nag, which isn't nice for me or the people around me and it makes them less likely to want to be around me and support me.

4. Who would I be without the thought?

Without the thought I would see clearly all the support I have. I would feel more grateful for the support I have and would reach out for help when I'm overburdened in a more effective way.

5. Turn the thought around:

I have great support!

Why is that true?

I have an amazing husband, amazing friends and family and a great childcare system in place. All I need to do is ask them for their help before I am in red brain.

Because the thoughts *I can't be late, I don't have enough time* and *I am not supported* (even though the last one manifested more as a feeling than a thought I was aware of) had been used so often they were strong and dominant pathways in my brain. My new insight alone did not erase those pathways, so the thoughts continued to pop up for some time. But now I did not have to believe the thoughts. I could greet them with kindness and then quickly ask myself, 'Is that true?' And then turn it around to *I have plenty of time* or *My time needs more of me* or *I am supported; all I need to do is ask*, which in time became my mantra in the form of 'Be here now' and 'You are not alone'.

Because I kept reminding myself that I have plenty of time I became much more relaxed and better able to plan and organize (it is so much easier in a green-brain state!). This literally resulted in me having more time. Because I started believing and feeling I am not alone but supported by great people, I started reaching out sooner in times of need, which only strengthened my relationships. Whatever you do, you always do it better from a green brain, so identifying the thoughts that activate the red brain and replacing them with thoughts that activate the green brain will make you more effective. The consequence is a calmer, kinder, happier you.

What if it doesn't work?

Finding the right stressful thought

It often takes some introspection and trying the technique on different thoughts before you get to the real core stressful thought. As with my example, you might start with a thought that is actually not at the core of the stress. Check in with yourself when you are feeling stressed, anxious or down, and monitor your thoughts without filtering them. What is the raw, unfiltered thought that creates a strong response in your body or emotions? That will often be the one you need to use for self-enquiry. Don't worry if you are struggling to find that core thought — this is work in progress. Just keep going, keep trying different thoughts until you find the one that really stands out.

Finding the right new thought

Feel free to play around with alternative thoughts. The direct turn-around is often just a starting point, and something will come up that really clicks with you. For example, my direct turn-around was 'I have enough time' but I then changed it into 'I have plenty of time'. 'Plenty' feels more abundant than 'enough' and therefore it is a stronger antidote to my core beliefs of there not being enough. Try out different ones until you find something that really clicks with you and gives you that feeling of relief.

Result comes with practice

It takes time and practice to change those stress-based pathways in your brain. Every time you practise this technique you are building and strengthening more helpful thoughts. It is useful to go through all the steps at least once, and I recommend that you write down each step and your answer. Beginning to practise the helpful thought takes conscious effort. The aim is to stick with it and *fake it till you make it*. In time these new and helpful thoughts will become your new automatic thoughts.

EXERCISE 5:
CHANGING STRESSFUL THOUGHTS

Use this technique on your recurring stressful thoughts.

STEP 1. Recurring stressful thought one.

1. Is it true? Yes or no? _____

2. Can you absolutely know that it is true? Yes or no? _____

3. How do you react, what happens, when you think that thought? What happens when you believe that thought? How do you feel? What does it make you want to do?

   _____

   _____

4. Who would you be without the thought? If tomorrow when you wake up, everything is the same but this thought has been erased from your mind, what would be different about you?

   _____

   _____

5. Turn the thought around.

Turn-around one.

Give three examples why that is true.

1. _____

2. _____

3. _____

Turn-around two.

Give three examples why that is true.

1. _____

2. _____

3. _____

Turn-around three.

Give three examples why that is true.

1. _____

2. _____

3. _____

STEP 2. Recurring stressful thought two.

1. Is it true? Yes or no? _____

2. Can you absolutely know that it is true? Yes or no? _____

3. How do you react when you think that thought? What happens when you believe that thought? How do you feel? What does it make you want to do?

    _____

    _____

4. Who would you be without the thought? If tomorrow when you wake up, everything is the same but this thought has been erased from your mind, what would be different about you?

    _____

    _____

5. Turn the thought around.

Turn-around one.

Give three examples why that is true.

1. _____
2. _____
3. _____

Turn-around two.

Give three examples why that is true.

1. _____
2. _____
3. _____

Turn-around three.

Give three examples why that is true.

1. _____
2. _____
3. _____

STEP 3. Recurring stressful thought two.

1. Is it true? Yes or no? _____

2. Can you absolutely know that it is true? Yes or no? _____

3. How do you react when you think that thought? What happens when you believe that thought? How do you feel? What does it make you want to do?

_____

_____

4. Who would you be without the thought? If tomorrow when you wake up, everything is the same but this thought has been erased from your mind, what would be different about you?

_____

_____

5. Turn the thought around.

Turn-around one.

Give three examples why that is true.

1. _____
2. _____
3. _____

Turn-around two.

Give three examples why that is true.

1. _____
2. _____
3. _____

Turn-around three.

Give three examples why that is true.

1. _____
2. _____
3. _____

RENEW YOUR MIND TIP

Replace every 'need' in your thoughts with 'would like to' and see what happens.

CHAPTER 7:

Mantras

It is likely that you are addicted to thinking. You think all day long; even when you have a moment of peace and quiet you will think of something to think of. It just never stops!

Your thoughts can be positive, neutral or negative. Negative thoughts push your brain towards the red part of the spectrum. When this happens everything that is not a priority for survival is put on hold. This includes learning, the development of skills and building of resources. When in the red zone, your brain's first priority is to make it through that moment.

Positive or neutral thoughts have the opposite effect: they allow you to stay in the green zone or return to green. This makes you more flexible, creative, better at problem-solving and more connected to the people around you. People with more positive thoughts are not only happier, they tend to have more success in life because their brain is better wired to learn, build skills and utilize resources, which makes them better at what they do.

Self-fulfilling prophecy

Positive thoughts have such an impact because they can become self-fulfilling prophecies. Sociologist Robert K. Merton first formalized this concept in 1948, describing it thus:

> The self-fulfilling prophecy is, in the beginning, a false definition of the situation evoking a new behaviour, which makes the originally false conception come true.

When you believe something negative to be true, you increase the likelihood for it to indeed come true because you are adjusting your brain activity and behaviour to meet your expectation. Remember that your brain does not react to how situations *are* but to how you *perceive* them to be. When you perceive a situation to be negative, the red brain kicks in, your attention narrows and your brain begins to scan the environment or your thoughts, looking for evidence that the perceived threat is indeed true. Your thoughts also influence your interpretation of what is happening around you, so it won't be long before you find your 'evidence' and can say to yourself, 'See, I knew this would happen.'

An example of a self-fulfilling prophecy is a fascinating experiment done by a brand of beauty products. In this experiment, two large signs were put above two identical, side-by-side doors. One sign said 'Beautiful' and the other sign said 'Average'. Women who wanted to enter the building had to enter through one of the two doors and they were unaware they were being filmed. It was interesting to see how many of these women chose the 'Average' door, but what was even more interesting to see was what it did to their beauty in that moment. The women who walked through the 'Average' door seemed more rushed, looked down and appeared closed off. The women who walked through the 'Beautiful' door walked slowly, with their heads up and often with a smile on their face. They looked confident, happy and open to connection. The women who believed, in that moment, that they were beautiful, became more beautiful because their posture and facial expression allowed their beauty to show. Nothing is more beautiful than a confident woman who is smiling.

One piece of advice you can take from the self-fulfilling prophecy concept is to never think or say anything about yourself that you don't want to come true. When you say things like, 'I am such a bad cook,' or 'My dog never listens to me,' or 'This is hard work,' or 'My partner doesn't love me enough,' it will change your brain state and response to the situation, making it truer than it was before you had the thought.

For example, if you think you are not a very good cook while you are cooking dinner it's more likely that you will make mistakes, become distracted and you will focus your attention on the things that go wrong rather than all the things that you do right. If you make a mistake your brain will say, *See, I knew I wasn't good at this!* This will colour your experience of the dinner and you will probably serve the food to your guests with an apology of some kind.

If, however, your thought was, *I'm going to cook a nice meal,* or *I'm a good cook,* your experience would be very different. If anything went wrong, you would not think it was a big deal and you would just fix it. You would not serve your meal while making apologies to your guests and they would not even notice little mistakes that you might have made.

Mental stress

Another relevant psychological concept is cognitive dissonance, also known as mental stress. First formalized by Leon Festinger, it focuses on the ways humans seek internal consistency. When you believe A, you will act according to A and look for evidence of A. When faced with evidence of B instead, internal mental stress is the result. Your brain always seeks to eliminate mental stress so it will either ignore the evidence for B or, if the evidence is strong enough, it will change its belief from A to B to confirm the thought to the reality and therefore eliminate the mental stress.

$$\text{Belief} + \begin{array}{c}\text{Contradicting}\\\text{evidence}\end{array} = \text{Mental stress}$$

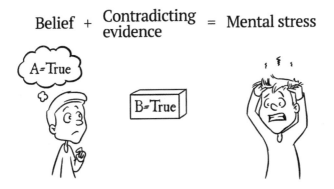

Ignore the evidence

Change your belief

For example, when you believe that others find you uninteresting, you will register every silence, every eye gaze and the number of times the person you are talking to looks away or checks their phone. You will analyze these neutral events and convince yourself they are evidence of your belief that you are uninteresting. The thought *I am uninteresting* will make you feel tense and self-conscious, which in turn could make you quiet and withdrawn. Thus your thought has shaped the reality, because silent and withdrawn people are rarely very interesting.

Thoughts become things

Understanding the powerful dynamics of the self-fulfilling prophecy and mental stress can make them tools you can use to your benefit. If thinking negative thoughts pushes your brain towards the red end of the spectrum, causing you to feel negative feelings and giving you negative outcomes, the opposite will happen if you think neutral or positive thoughts.

If you think neutral or positive thoughts, your brain activity will move towards the green end of the spectrum, making you feel more optimistic and creating more positive outcomes. Remember, your thoughts are the most powerful tool you have in reshaping your brain and reshaping your happiness.

Mindful thinking versus positive thinking

Mindfulness is staying in the moment and connecting with that moment, as it is, in a neutral and kind way. Positive thinking is creating positive expectations that shape your outcomes and your reality. They are complementary approaches that work in different ways.

This is a simplification of a complex reality, but it can be a useful tool in understanding the power of thoughts. In a table it looks like this:

NEGATIVE THOUGHTS	MINDFULNESS	POSITIVE THOUGHTS
Negative beliefs	Neutral beliefs	Positive beliefs
Red brain	Orange/green brain	Green brain
Negative feelings	Neutral/positive feelings	Positive feelings
Looking for evidence that the negative belief is true	Observing the facts	Looking for evidence that the positive belief is true
Negative behaviours	Neutral/positive behaviours	Neutral/positive behaviours
Negative outcomes	Neutral/positive outcomes	Neutral/positive outcomes
Negative belief is confirmed	Neutral belief is confirmed or a positive surprise	Positive belief is confirmed

Imagine you wake up in the morning. You are still in bed, still sleepy and you realize you have a big day ahead of you. Today is the day you will present your ideas to the rest of your team and they will give you feedback. Then one of these three thoughts pops into your mind: *Today is going to be dreadful*, or *Today will be okay*, or *Today is going to be great!* This is how these three thoughts could influence you and your day.

Thought	Today is going to be dreadful	Today will be okay	Today is going to be great!
Brain state	Red brain	Orange/green brain	Green brain
Feeling	You feel stressed, down and agitated	You feel nervous	You feel confident and positive
Perception (glasses)	You interpret events negatively	You interpret events neutrally	You interpret events positively
Behaviour	You are withdrawn and cranky	You are focused but able to connect	You are open, receptive and chatty
Consequences short-term	People avoid you, you make mistakes and feel unsupported	People are neutral but open towards you, you perform well and feel connected	People are drawn to you, you perform well and feel connected and supported
Outcome	It has become a dreadful day	It has become an okay/good day	It has become a great day

Most people have negative thinking habits, and to jump to positive thinking habits can feel inauthentic. The risk associated with taking such a big step is that the new thoughts won't last. The key for it to work is to come up with thoughts that feel real and authentic to you.

Mantra

The word mantra comes from Sanskrit and means:

> 'A word or group of words that are believed by someone to have spiritual or psychological power. It is also described as "That which protects the mind".'
> — Jan Gonda

The beauty of an affirmation mantra is that it helps keep you on track with your practice. It is a mental reminder of your goals and mental exercise at the same time. You can practise a mantra at any time, anywhere, and the more you practise it the more it becomes part of your automatic thoughts. The more you think it, the more it shapes your reality.

For example, if your goal is to eat healthier food, one of the things that can help your mind to stay on track with this goal is to use the mantra, 'I eat healthy food'. If you say this to yourself on a regular basis you are more likely to eat healthier foods. If you use the mantra and continue to eat unhealthy food, the discrepancy between your thoughts and your actions will lead to mental stress and one of two things will happen: you will begin to make healthier food choices or you will stop using the mantra. Both options will eliminate the mental stress. Therefore, if you stick with your mantra and use it on a daily basis you are increasing the likelihood of reaching your goal.

Mindful affirmations

A mantra or mindful affirmation is an effective tool to help train your mind to have more green-brain thoughts. An effective way to create a mantra is to first think about your goals: what do you want to achieve today, this week or this year? Then, based on your goals, choose one or more sentences that help you stay on track with your goals.

Here are some examples.

GOAL	MANTRA
To become more confident.	'Actually, I can!'
To be kinder to your partner.	'Today I want to make my partner feel loved.'

GOAL	MANTRA
To create more fun times with your kids.	'In this house we have fun!'
To relax more.	'I make time to take care of my mind and my body.'
To clear your to-do list.	'By the end of this week my to-do list will be completed.'
Learning to say no.	'This week I will practise my "no".'
To be more positive	'Today will be a good day.'

The exercise on the following page shows you a mantra I use regularly. It sets me up for a mindful day and helps me to stay on track with my goal of living mindfully. You can try the entire mantra or just a part that stands out to you. Remember repetition is key, so be strategic about how you will practise your mantra.

EXERCISE 6:
MINDFULNESS MANTRA

I am kind and non-judgmental, open, curious and confident. I stop arguing with the facts and I accept what is so I can free my mind to make the changes I want to make.

I eat good food and take good care of my body. I sleep well and take time to rest and have fun. I am aware of my body and I appreciate it and what it does for me.

I choose to be aware and conscious and take time every day to be in the here and now. I choose to be mindful of my emotions and process them instead of suppressing them or becoming stuck in them.

I am aware of my thinking, and that it is not the events but my thoughts that cause me stress. I turn my stressful thoughts around and choose thoughts that are helpful to me.

I let go of things that hold me back, I accept what has happened and I let it go so I can be free.

I am grateful for my life and the people in it. I keep my goals in mind and I go confidently in the direction of my dreams.

RENEW YOUR MIND TIP

Write down your mantra and put it where you'll see it often: in your wallet, on your mirror or as your phone screensaver. Every time you see it you'll read it and will have done another exercise.

CHAPTER 8:

The mind–body connection

We have already looked at different ways you can change your thoughts to become effective green-brain activators, making you happier, healthier and more balanced. In this chapter we will look at simple, practical ways you can adjust your body to achieve that same goal.

Your mind and your body are important parts of your being, of who you are. Some see them as separate elements (the dualistic approach), and others consider the mind and the body to be one and the same thing (monistic approach). Whatever your preferred approach, it is fair to say that the mind and the body are both important. More and more research shows that the mind and the body influence each other significantly and that this pathway is a two-way street.

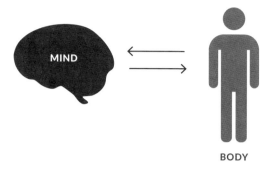

How the mind influences the body

Your mind influences your body and its physical processes. A simple way to experience this is to close your eyes and take as little as 30 seconds to think about a situation that is causing you stress. Do you notice the immediate increase in tension in your muscles, the change in breathing and heart rate? Most people also experience tightness in their chest or their stomach. All of this is a direct result of the release of the stress hormones adrenaline and cortisol. That is how quickly your thoughts change what is happening in your body.

When you are able to control your stressful thoughts and turn them around to helpful, green-brain thoughts, your body will release stress-reducing hormones and your muscle tension, heart rate and blood pressure will decrease. Take a moment to close your eyes and think back to a very happy time in your life. See yourself and the people who were there. Do you notice the immediate relaxation in your muscles, your shoulders dropping and your breathing slowing down? Most people will even begin to smile when they recall a happy memory. Just as thinking about a stressful situation quickly increases stress, thinking about a positive situation reduces stress and increases happiness.

How the body influences the mind

Because the mind–body connection is a two-way street, your body also influences your mind. One clear example of this is the significantly increased risk of developing depression or other mood disorders when a physical illness is present. Our physical health and the way we move our body influences the mind. Research by Professor Beilock of the University of Chicago shows that the way we move affects our thoughts, our decisions and even our preferences for particular products. Beilock also found that pacing around a room can enhance creativity, gesturing during a speech can help ensure that you don't draw a blank, kids learn better when their bodies are part of the learning process, walking in nature boosts concentration, and the use of Botox eases depression because it prevents people from frowning.

Posture

Your body can influence your mind through posture. To experience the significance of how your posture affects your mind, sit in a hunched over, curled-up position for 1 minute. Notice the immediate effect this change in posture has on how you think and feel. Most people immediately begin to feel uncomfortable, anxious or nervous, indicating they are moving to the unsafe part of the spectrum which is red brain. The opposite is also true. When you sit or stand tall, release the tension from your neck and shoulder area and hold your chin up, you will feel more confident and capable because you are moving towards the green part of the spectrum where you feel safe.

Your mind is constantly 'reading' your posture and adjusting how it thinks and feels based on the cues it receives. Hunching over, looking towards the floor and making yourself small sends a powerful signal to your brain that you are not feeling safe and confident. The mind picks up on that signal and it activates the orange- or red-brain state, making stress levels go up.

Facial expressions

Facial expressions are another powerful tool to change how you think and feel. To experience this, take a pen and put it horizontally between your teeth, forcing a fake smile. This will seem fake and odd but pay attention to how it makes you feel. Most people experience an immediate reduction of stress and increase of happiness by smiling.

Even if the smile is not genuine, it will still affect your mood as your mind is constantly 'reading' your face and adjusting how it thinks and feels based on the cues it receives. Your mouth and eyebrows are especially important messengers to the brain. Simply changing your facial expression to represent the mind state you want to achieve — in this case a green-brain, relaxed and happy state — will lead to a quick and significant shift towards the desired state.

Another interesting phenomenon you can test while you have the pen in your mouth creating a fake smile is to try to think about something stressful or negative. You will notice that it's very difficult to bring negative things to mind when you are smiling. Your facial expression 'locks' your brain in the brain state it is linked to, making it hard to access thoughts and feelings that are linked to other states. You can use this to your advantage by staying aware of your facial expressions and trying to keep your expression relaxed and positive. Try to notice when you're frowning, then relax your eyebrows and, if you can, create a little smile. Your brain and mood will follow.

Taking up space

In the animal kingdom there is a clear link between taking up space and dominance. This link is part of our DNA too. When we feel powerful in the moment or long term we tend to naturally take up more space by making ourselves bigger: by standing tall, holding our chin up and making our shoulders broad. In challenging moments this will happen by making large gestures and raising our chin even higher. In moments of pride and victory, such as winning a race or a game, the universal response, even in people born blind, is to raise our arms high in the air. The fact that blind people demonstrate this response too shows that it isn't learned but rather is a tendency that is programmed into our minds and is part of our subconscious way of responding when we feel powerful.

When we feel powerless or unconfident we do the opposite; we make ourselves small by hunching over, crossing our arms and legs and looking down (or at our phone). We avoid taking up space and make ourselves small in order to protect ourselves.

More research

Psychologist Amy Cuddy from the University of Chicago studied the link between posture and confidence levels. She and her colleagues found that, just as they expected, people who feel confident have low levels of cortisol (the stress hormone) and high levels of testosterone (the confidence and dominance hormone).

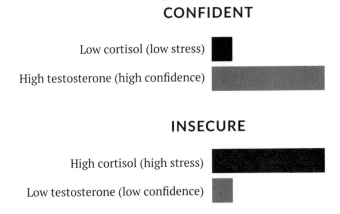

CONFIDENT

Low cortisol (low stress)

High testosterone (high confidence)

INSECURE

High cortisol (high stress)

Low testosterone (low confidence)

They combined this knowledge with studies that were done on apes and found that when a less dominant ape takes over the role of the alpha male, it takes only a few days for him to start both looking and behaving more dominantly. The change of role affects the ape's posture and his behaviour, and most likely his levels of cortisol and testosterone change accordingly.

Amy Cuddy and her team were interested to find out if the same change in role could achieve that result in humans. They did a double-blind study where the participants had to attend a stressful job interview. One group of participants did a 2-minute power pose — for example, standing tall with fists resting on the side of the body (the Wonder Woman pose) — before the interview. The other group was told to do a low-power pose — for example, sitting hunched over and looking at the floor — for the same amount of time.

The results showed that a 2-minute power pose was followed by a 20 per cent increase in testosterone and a 25 per cent decrease in cortisol. A submissive pose led to a 10 per cent decrease in testosterone and 15 per cent increase in cortisol.

People who were asked to do the power pose felt more confident and capable, and their hormone levels reflected this. Even more surprisingly, without exception, the people who performed the power pose were rated by the people conducting the job interview as more capable, more likeable and better suited for the job. This outcome was independent of the participant's skill set and background. It shows that confident participants perform significantly better socially, which can lead to important benefits such as being hired for a job.

A 2-minute power pose, however, does not make you a nicer person or improve your skill set. It is more likely that by doing a 2-minute power pose you are preventing the red-brain state from kicking in and hijacking your brain. When your brain is in the red zone and you are highly stressed, it is unlikely you will be able to connect well to others and to show them the real and most likeable and capable you. When stress takes over, you simply cannot be your authentic self and others pick up on that. Doing a power pose allows you to stay on top of your stress so you can show them the best version of you and connect with people in a more natural and authentic way.

The mind of the powerful

A person with low levels of cortisol (low stress) and high testosterone levels (high confidence) is in the green- or orange-brain state and feels confident and optimistic. This leads to assertive responses and more risk-taking. This pattern is also found in powerful and effective leaders and can hugely impact your success both at home and at work.

A person with high cortisol levels (high stress) and low testosterone levels (low confidence) is in the red-brain state and feels quickly overwhelmed and stressed. In this state of stress you cannot perform at your best. This subtle but important change can make the difference between a promotion or no promotion, speaking up about injustice or remaining silent, or managing a chaotic household while keeping your cool or yelling at your kids and then regretting your actions.

When we observe posture and how it changes to reflect changes in mood and the accompanied hormones in our system, we see an interesting pattern emerge. The amount of stress determines how much space the body takes up, with confidence being a mitigating factor. When confidence is low and stress is high, red brain is activated and you are likely to feel either scared (loss of control, flight response) or angry (attempt to get control back, fight response). When you feel scared or anxious you will make yourself smaller. The more scared you are the smaller you will make yourself. Your posture reflects your emotion and the hormone balance that produces the emotion. This posture signals surrender and submission to the person or situation that is triggering the fear. When confidence is added, stress is reduced, allowing you to move out of red-brain fear or orange-brain anxiety into calm assertive. When even more confidence is added you move into the confident, active assertive role. This is reflected by a posture that stands tall and takes up more space by taking on a power pose. Both calm assertive and active assertive are part of the green-brain zone. We see it playing out in the body by taking up even more space. When you are faced with a stress-triggering threat while being able to keep your brain out of the red zone you are tapping into the state of courage. However, if you are uncertain of victory, stress levels will remain high, which results in your body becoming smaller but your confidence and willingness to take on the challenge will keep you out of red-brain fear or anger. At the opposite end of the spectrum we find reactive aggression, which might look confident and dominant, but having to resort to aggression shows a lack of confidence and control and a red-brain state. Again, this is reflected in the body language.

SUBMISSIVE   CALM   ACTIVE   COURAGEOUS AGGRESSIVE
              ASSERTIVE   ASSERTIVE

Mindfulness of the body

Understanding the powerful link between posture and facial expression and red and green brain allows you to take control over your brain state through consciously adjusting your body and face to ensure you stay in the green zone or return to it. You can do this in several ways.

When you find yourself on the left of the green zone (the anxious red brain), the power pose is a great way to quickly reduce stress and boost your confidence levels in the moment. This brings your system back to the green zone. When you are at risk of ending up in red-brain anger, consciously take on the assertive posture by standing tall with relaxed shoulders and facial muscles. This will help your brain return to green, where you are back in control of what you do and say. As I said in Chapter 1, red brain is the emergency brain which is also reflected in this model. Even when we are under pressure, green brain has available the full range of calm assertive to strong and active courage, enabling us to deal with whatever comes our way. Learning how to cultivate and train confidence is a big part of learning how to do everyday life in green brain.

A way to increase overall confidence is to be mindfully aware of your body. Making changes to your posture and facial expression begins with checking in with your body and auditing it on a regular basis. All it takes is a moment of bringing your awareness to your body and how you are holding it. If you notice you are in a low-power pose, simply adjust your posture by taking up more space. Try the following.

» Uncross your legs (also better for circulation).

» Unwrap your arms.

» Sit up straight without straining your upper back.

» Broaden your shoulders.

» Lift your chin.

» Smile ☺.

If you are at risk of moving to red brain anger, the following posture adjustments can help bring you back to green:

» Sit or lie down.

» Relax your shoulders.

» Relax your hands (laying them down with your palms up can be a quick way to do this).

» Relax your facial muscles.

» Slow down your breathing.

EXERCISE 7:
BOOSTING CONFIDENCE

To experience a quick and strong boost in confidence, try the power pose by following these steps.

STEP 1. Think of something you have to do or want to achieve, something you do not feel very confident about. This can be anything from sorting out your administration, to painting a fence, to making a meal plan or writing an article.

I want to: _____

STEP 2. Score your confidence level regarding this particular goal on a scale of 1 to 10, with 1 being not confident at all and 10 being very confident.

Confidence level: _____

STEP 3. Stand up, set your alarm for 2 minutes and do a power pose. Lift your hands in the air, hold your chin up and make it a powerful pose full of energy.

STEP 4. The power pose is even more effective when at the same time you envision yourself winning or succeeding at something. You could envision yourself accomplishing a particular goal you have in mind or you can think back to past successful experiences.

When your arms get sore, just notice it in a kind and non-judgmental way and turn your attention back to that image of you winning or succeeding. Try to keep the pose strong and energetic until the 2 minutes are up.

STEP 5. Now think back to the task or goal you rated before you did the pose, and rate your level of confidence again. How confident do you feel now about accomplishing this task or reaching this goal?

Confidence level: _____

Most people will experience an increase of 2–5 points on their confidence scale, which is pretty amazing considering the fact that this exercise takes only 2 minutes.

How to apply the power pose in daily life

The power pose is a perfect confidence booster when you are about to go into a challenging situation such as a job interview, a difficult meeting or when going shopping with children. Whenever you are about to do something and you cannot afford to let stress take over, this is a quick and helpful tool that will give you a boost in energy and confidence. However, the increase in confidence only lasts for 15 to 30 minutes. Therefore, I recommend combining regular practice of the power pose with practising general mindfulness of your posture and facial expression. By combining the two you will have the benefits of the quick peaks of confidence that the power pose gives as well as the overall increase in confidence that comes from a good and open posture. In time, you will establish a new base rate of confidence and it won't require any conscious attention.

For example, one of my course participants listened to this explanation of how posture affects the mind and replied by saying, 'This is true, I did this!' She shared with the group how she was anxious and suicidal at the age of sixteen. Then she decided she had to do something. She decided to start faking being confident. She observed confident people and copied their posture, their way of moving and talking. It felt very inauthentic but according to her anything was better than how she had been feeling. After a couple of months she was no longer suicidal and her extreme insecurity had gone. She had become more confident. She faked being confident until she had become it.

 ## RENEW YOUR MIND TIP

A good, confident posture and a smile is my number-one technique to keep stress under control and deliver a good performance or presentation.

CHAPTER 9:

Creating success and happiness

There are various myths that focus on achievement and happiness, believed by many and helpful to few. Let's explore the truth about the most common of these myths.

The happiness myth

The happiness myth is the idea that being mindful equals being calm and happy always. Living mindfully, however, does not mean that you are happy or content all the time, nor does it mean striving to reach a state of constant bliss and happiness. Life would be pretty flat and boring if it were devoid of any stirring emotions. The more green-brain activity, the more happiness you will have in your life, but there will still be moments of sadness, fear and even anger. The big difference is that these moments are no longer unbearable. They have become manageable and you can see the value of any event and emotion. You have become comfortable riding the waves of emotions caused by life, because you have become a skilled surfer. With a trained mind you can process the emotions, take helpful action and return to a state of green-brain happiness.

Doing everyday life in green brain means that you aim to be present with whatever happens. You observe the event, thought or emotion in a kind and non-judgmental way, which will activate your green brain. You can still feel sad, frustrated or insecure, but when you are in the green zone these feelings are not overwhelming and you remain in the driver's seat. There is a sense of calm and control and you are responsive instead of reactive. It could mean the difference between yelling at your partner for doing something wrong or explaining to them how important something is to you. It can be the difference between creating even more resistance in a difficult staff member or getting them back on track. It could be the difference between a stress-induced heart attack at age 60 or a long and happy life well into your nineties.

The stress = success myth

The success myth is another common myth, closely linked to the productivity myth that I covered in Chapter 1. Many people believe you need stress in order to be motivated, productive and successful. The stressed-out employee who does the most hours is seen as the most motivated and dedicated and gets the badge of honour. It's assumed stress and success go hand in hand. It is a myth because stress activates the red brain, which makes it more difficult to achieve your goals (unless your goal is to fight a bear or run from a fire). So, stress and especially stressful thoughts are not as helpful to you as you might think.

I believe this misunderstanding stems in part from equating mental labour to physical labour. If you work in a factory at an assembly line it is true that the harder you work and the more hours you do the greater the output. But when it comes to mental work that involves creative thinking, social skills, problem-solving skills etc., this logic simply doesn't apply. Your brain and muscles have different requirements for optimal output but conflating the two leads us to believe the stress = success myth.

When you begin to understand your brain, and accept that creating *physical* output works differently from creating *mental* output, you will learn to trust your brain more. Just as your immune system is programmed to tirelessly fight viruses and bad bacteria and keep you healthy at all times, your brain is programmed to help you achieve your goals. When you create the right conditions and combine your green brain with a clearly defined goal or purpose, you can trust that your brain will help you achieve those goals. You don't need stress to keep you moving forward. In green brain, it is motivation, values and an in-built desire for improvement and progress that will drive the engine, not stress. This will preserve your happiness and your health and lead to success. With stress as the driving force, you might be successful but you will damage your health and happiness in the process.

From my own experience, I can testify that it is also true that what I achieve in green brain is more efficient and of a higher quality than what I can achieve in red brain. In green brain, I am able to notice what isn't working and rethink my approach. In red brain, I tend to just keep going and believe that the solution to the lack of progress is to work harder. In green brain, I am better able to focus while in red brain I waste more time procrastinating and thinking about working without actually getting into it and getting things done. As Tim Urban puts it in his excellent TED talk on procrastination, we procrastinate until we look at the clock and realize we don't have enough time, which wakes up the panic monster (red brain) in us and that is when we get to work.

In green brain, I notice when my brain needs a break and I take a proper break to refresh my brain. In red brain, I keep going for too long and take 'breaks' that usually consist of online snacking on useless content that does nothing to refresh my brain and boost my productivity.

Isn't it ironic that when red brain achieves its goal after all that procrastination, panic-monster-induced hard work, and lack of real breaks, it receives a shot of dopamine and tells itself 'This is the proof that stress really does lead to success!'

Even when people say they don't believe that stress equals success, I have caught many of them believing that if they haven't worked hard, stressed out and done long hours to achieve something, it isn't really an achievement. They subconsciously measure the accomplishment by the suffering they endured to get there not by the outcome. If it was fun and ideas and output came easily they are less likely to see it as a success no matter the quality of the work they produced.

I keep the 'working hard' gear available for exceptions and 'work emergencies' but, as a rule, when I'm working from red brain it is a sign that something is very wrong. I need to stop what I am doing and find my way back to green brain before I can continue my work. Since I have started implementing these insights into my work life, our company has doubled in size and tripled in revenue. Grit is important — being able to push through when you need to is necessary to be successful — but when you begin to reward working smart over working hard, a lot will change for the better.

When you stress less, you achieve more.

Present-moment awareness

You don't realize how much time you are wasting until you become aware of the present moment. Because of the way our society works — education, work structures, internet, phones, entertainment, advertising — a state of non-presence has become normal. Most of the time we are distracted and think about the next thing instead of what is happening right now and we have come to believe that this is a good thing. In turn, we have also come to believe that as soon as we slow down we are slacking off and then 'the fear of missing out' kicks in.

Most people seem to be constantly looking for something that will transport them into happiness. Happiness that they believe is in the future. When you tie your happiness to a future goal you believe you cannot be fully satisfied until that goal is accomplished. Physically you are living in the now but your mind is occupied with the future. Your mind is in a state of waiting until 'your happiness' arrives. In reality you are postponing your happiness and are not able to see and enjoy all the wonderful things that are happening in the now. Then at some point, you reach your goal and feel a sense of achievement, happiness and relief. This feeling lasts for some time but soon you will find yourself tying your happiness to yet another goal.

'I'm so happy with our new kitchen, isn't it amazing? But we really need to do something about the living room. Once the living room is done I'll be so happy.' (Of course there will be another renovation job to be done after that.)

'I made it through this week of deadlines, what a relief! But the next project really needs to start soon. When that is done I can finally have some down time.' (Of course there will be another important project waiting.)

'When we have an income of $100,000 a year we will be comfortable and life will be great.' (Of course by the time you have reached the milestone of earning $100,000 a year you will have adjusted your lifestyle and you will need $150,000 a year to be 'comfortable'.)

As Eckhart Tolle points out:

> 'The future always comes as the now, therefore if you cannot be happy in the now you will never be happy.'

For many people it feels wrong to be present in the now and fully enjoy it, as if being present and content should be a reward for hard work and achievements. There is a belief that the contentment should not last too long or you will become lazy. With this mindset, happiness does not come from life, it comes from achievements and you believe that if you allow yourself too much happiness you will not move forward in life.

The truth is that you are reducing your productivity by not allowing yourself to be present in the now. By always striving for the next thing you are damaging your brain, your body, your relationships and your success. Your motivation does not depend on your stress and if it does you should wonder if you are chasing a goal that is worth chasing. When you are not present, when you allow your mind to constantly wander off into the future and focus on the things that you will gain there, you lose sight of all the wonderful moments and things that are happening all around you. Who knows what will happen in the future? All you have is the now. When your mind is occupied with the future you are living in a world that does not exist yet and you cannot enjoy or function to your full potential in the now.

Just imagine how freeing it would be to stop believing that you need future goals and achievements to complete your happiness. To believe that you are exactly where you need to be in life and that it is not about the end goal but about what you do with the now or, as Alan Watts puts it, 'In music, though, one doesn't make the end of the composition the point of the composition. If that were so, the best conductors would be those who played fastest; and there would be composers who only wrote finales. People would go to concerts only to hear one crashing chord—because that's the end. Same way in dancing— you don't aim at a particular spot in the room; that's where you should arrive. The whole point of the dancing is the dance ...'.

INSIGHT INSPIRATION

1. To what future goal/achievement are you tying your happiness?

    _____

    _____

    _____

    _____

2. If everything else stayed the same but you allowed yourself to be fully present and happy in the now, what would be different?

    _____

    _____

    _____

    _____

    _____

3. What would you do differently?

    _____

    _____

    _____

    _____

4. How would that make you feel?

    _____

    _____

    _____

    _____

Gratitude

An effective and fun way to increase present-moment happiness is by practising gratitude. Practising gratitude is nothing more than redirecting your focus from possible good things of the future to the good things of the now.

You can practise gratitude anytime and anywhere, but for your initial practice I recommend dedicating a specific moment of your day. You can simply think about the things you are grateful for, but writing them down will increase the impact of the exercise. Sharing with your partner, a friend or your children what you are grateful for is a great way to increase mindful connection.

EXERCISE 8: GRATITUDE

STEP 1. Take a moment to think about your life and what you have to be grateful for.

For example: I am grateful to be alive. I am grateful for my health, for my body that works for me every single day. I am grateful for my mind that allows me to think and be me, I am grateful for . . .

STEP 2. Be grateful for your partner or a close friend.

Picture this person, their whole body or just their face. What is it about them that you love? What things about their personality do you appreciate? What do you like about the way they look? What do they do for you that you can be grateful for? In your mind thank them for being part of your life.

STEP 3. Be grateful for a child in your life.

Picture this child, as if they were standing right in front of you. What is it about them that you love? What do you like about how they look? About what they do? How do they make you feel? Then thank them for being part of your life.

STEP 4. Be grateful for your family and friends.

Picture them all or one person in particular, envision what they look like and imagine they are right there standing before you. Take a moment to think about specific things about your family as a whole or about a particular family member. What do you like about your family? What does your family do for you that you can be grateful for? How does that make you feel? Then, in your mind, thank them for being part of your life.

STEP 5. Is there anyone else in your life that you can be grateful for?

Picture that person, their whole body or just their face. What is it about them that you like? What do they do for you that you can be grateful for? How do they make you feel? And then, thank them for being part of your life and for who they are and what they do for you.

STEP 6. What things can you be grateful for? Even if they are not perfect or exactly what you want?

Are you grateful for your house? Can you be grateful for your means of transportation? Can you be grateful for the money you have? For your job or for the opportunity to take time off? What do you have in your life to be grateful for? Picture those things in front of you and express your gratitude for them.

But how do we move forward?

Many people are high achievers and have big dreams and visions for their future. They might have goals such as starting a family, building a house, finding an amazing job or building a business. Often they can see the value of present-moment happiness and they have experienced first-hand how constantly chasing achievements burns them out. They feel that something is missing but don't trust that present-moment happiness will help them achieve their goals.

Green-brain mindful awareness activates present-moment happiness and also creative thinking, energized focus, motivation and big dreams and visions. Therefore, mindfulness is not just the starting point of moving forward, it is also the fuel that keeps you going.

The model of Flow proposed by Vishen Lakhiani states there are four states you can be in: a negative spiral, current-reality trap, stress or flow. According to this model, the state you are in depends on two factors: present-moment happiness and future vision.

YOUR STATE	PRESENT-MOMENT HAPPINESS	CLEAR GOAL / VISION
Negative spiral	NO	NO
Current-reality trap	YES	NO
Stress	NO	YES
Flow	YES	YES

Negative spiral

If you are not happy in the now and are also not working towards a particular goal or vision, you find yourself in a state called 'negative spiral'. You have negative thoughts and feelings and no direction or plan to take you out of this place of negativity. You feel trapped in your situation and believe you lack the resources and skills to change it. This state comes with low levels of self-esteem and energy. Being stuck in a negative spiral can lead to depressive symptoms.

If you are in a negative spiral, not happy in the now and have no goals to work towards, the green-brain techniques can feel useless. If you feel this way, remind yourself that research shows that training your brain changes the neural pathways in your brain. It might feel like hard work, but regular practice in these techniques is just as effective in reshaping your brain as regular workouts are effective in building physical strength. One client found herself trapped in a negative spiral. She is a single mother who recovered from a severe drug addiction and was unable to find a job. She had low energy levels, was overweight and believed that there was no point in trying to make any changes because so far all her attempts had failed. Most days she would go back to bed after dropping her son at school and she would eat large amounts of junk food to feel somewhat better, only to feel worse afterwards. The green-brain techniques made her grow in present-moment awareness. Practising gratitude helped her see the many things she had to be grateful for (and all the successful changes she had already made!). She became grateful for the good things in her life such as regaining custody of her son and being drug-free for more than four years. Focusing on these achievements instilled hope that she would be able to convince someone to hire her. She reconnected with her passion for children and was able to convince the head teacher of her son's school to offer her an internship while she began to study to become a certified teacher's assistant. Now she is studying and working part-time in a job that allows her to assist autistic children — and she loves it.

She is a wonderful example of how becoming happier in the now, by focusing on the good things you already have and seeing how you have accomplished them, opens up a world of possibilities. This change made her grow in self-esteem and reconnect with her passion for children, which created a future vision of working as a teacher's assistant. With both present-moment happiness and a future vision in place, she made a plan and executed it successfully.

Current-reality trap

In the current-reality trap you are happy in the now but you have no goals or vision for the future. This sounds like a fun place to be, and it is — at least in the short term. This is where many people fear they will end up if they were to let go of the belief that happiness comes from achievements. However, research shows that to reach a place of deeper happiness and fulfilment we need achievements and growth. The need for growth is part of the human fabric, which is reflected in the brain. There is a whole set of 'happy chemicals' reserved for that kind of happiness.

The current-reality trap can lead to stalled motivation and growth due to a lack of goals and future vision. This then leads to superficial happiness and is usually not sustainable in the long term. It often goes hand in hand with addictions because they are shortcuts to a yes in the 'Happy in the now' box. But addictions don't create sustainable happiness that leads to achievements and growth.

If you are stuck in the current-reality trap you probably won't see the need for change until the costs of your situation begin to outweigh the benefits. If this happens, remind yourself that regular practice is effective in changing patterns and finding ways that are more fulfilling.

For example, a client who is a nineteen-year-old student would game for hours on end and was really happy when he was doing this. He did not see any problem with gaming for eight hours every day. When his parents divorced and sold the house he was forced to look for a flat; he became overwhelmed with social fears and insecurities. Years of gaming had taken its toll on his mental and emotional growth, his social skills and resilience in the face of change. His excessive gaming had him caught in the current-reality trap where he was happy while he was gaming but overcome by stress in the real world.

Through therapy he was able to see that gaming had left him several years behind in his social development. Most of his peers had struggled with the same things he was struggling with, but they overcame it years ago. As he saw that his fears made perfect sense, his goal became to overcome his social fears. Together we made a game plan, but this time it was about how to succeed in social situations. His love for games remained but he now also had real goals and a vision for his future. Towards the end of the therapy he found a flat with people who shared his love for gaming. He now has a part-time job in a retirement home and spends his weekends socializing without being overcome by social anxiety. He conquered his crippling fears and lives a life that is fulfilling in several ways, not just one.

A state of stress

You end up in a state of stress when you are not happy in the now and you have big dreams and goals for the future. In a state of stress, there is a pressure to move forward to reach these goals, which you believe will make you happy, yet there is no happiness to fuel the move forward. This is not a problem if it lasts for a short while, but when it occurs often or lasts too long, it will cause damage to your brain and the rest of your body, which eventually can lead to burnout.

In a state of stress you are trying to reach your goals but because you have tied your happiness to these goals you are putting your brain in the red- or the orange-brain state. You are trying to reach your goal with a brain state that blocks creative thinking, problem-solving and flexibility. This makes it so much harder to actually reach your goals and you end up feeling frustrated, drained and disappointed.

If you are in the state of stress and start to practise the green-brain techniques, you might feel uncomfortable and restless because it feels like you are wasting time and the fear of missing out will show up. However, hold on to the fact that spending only a few minutes per day on activating the ideal brain state for achievement — the green brain — will not only make you feel better, it will make you more effective and efficient. This will save more time than it has cost you and will help you reach your goals.

For example, one client used to live in the state of stress. She had a great life with friends, family, a beautiful house by the beach, a fantastic job and plenty of resources. Yet she felt as if life could not 'start', she could not be happy, until she had a partner. This made her unable to enjoy all the wonderful things she already had. Over time, it made her frustrated and angry and her sole focus became finding a life partner. This took all the relaxation and fun out of socializing, which did not make her very attractive to the men she was dating.

She ended up feeling exhausted and burned out, as if she was living her life running on a treadmill without ever reaching her destination. Her way out of this unhelpful dynamic was to 'step off the treadmill' and learn to appreciate and enjoy life just as it was. In time she began to see that life did not have to be perfect to be good, and we can have unfulfilled dreams and goals and still be happy and grateful in the now.

A state of flow

When you are happy in the now and you also have dreams and visions for the future you are tapping into what researchers call a state of flow. When you are in flow, your present-moment awareness activates the green brain, and then adding clear goals to this makes your efforts directed, efficient and focused. You will not only be happier but also more successful in achieving your goal because you are operating from the ideal brain state: the green brain. You are not letting your happiness depend on your achievements but you use your present-moment happiness to fuel your next achievements. In other words: allowing yourself to be happy in the now, no matter what the now is like, is not just about being happy, it is about being smart and creating the ideal circumstances for improvements to happen.

> The more you can enjoy and be happy in the now, the better your future will be.

When we combine the brain states and the model of flow we see this:

YOUR STATE	PRESENT-MOMENT HAPPINESS	BRAIN STATE	CLEAR GOAL/ VISION	LIKELIHOOD OF SUCCESS
Negative spiral	NO	⚡⚡⚡	NO	LOW
Current-reality trap	YES	≈	NO	LOW
Stress	NO	⚡⚡⚡	YES	LOW
Flow	YES	≈	YES	HIGH

Flow can be a way of life that is a result of being happy in the now and having a clear goal or vision for your life; it can also be defined as a momentary brain state. Psychologist Mihaly Csíkszentmihályi is a leading researcher when it comes to the momentary state of flow. He defines this state as:

'The mental state of operation in which a person performing an activity is fully immersed in a feeling of energized focus, full involvement, and enjoyment in the process of the activity. In essence, flow is characterized by complete absorption in what one does.'

Flow and the brain

Some interesting things happen in the brain when this momentary state of flow is activated. The activity in the prefrontal cortex, the part of the brain that functions as the central executive or the control room, is temporarily reduced. This part of the brain organizes and filters information in efficient and orderly ways to prevent your system from becoming overwhelmed. Having an active control room allows you to function in everyday life. However, when the activity in the prefrontal cortex is temporarily reduced, the rational and judgmental part of the brain is reduced and the more emotional and primal parts take over. This state resembles the brain activity that occurs when you are daydreaming or are about to fall asleep. In this almost 'hypnotic state' thoughts flow freely and links are made that you were not able to make with your conscious thinking. This state of free-flowing ideas, thoughts and images is at the core of creativity.

The difference between daydreaming and flow is that flow comes with increased focus. It releases a neurochemical cocktail in the brain that allows you to absorb more information. The increased creativity and focus combined make the state of flow the ideal brain state for creative thinking, innovation and problem-solving.

Putting it into practice

There are two important things that contribute to activating the state of flow. The first one is a good balance between the difficulty of the task and your skills: if the task is too easy you might become bored and lose focus; if the task is too difficult you become stressed, which also blocks flow.

As Csíkszentmihályi puts it:

> 'Flow happens naturally when a person's skills are fully involved in overcoming a challenge that is just about manageable. If challenges are too low, one gets back to flow by increasing them. If challenges are too great, one can return to the flow state by learning new skills.'

The second key element of the state of flow is focus. Having a strong focus requires you to be fully present with what you are doing without being distracted by external factors (such as multitasking or constantly checking your phone) or internal factors (such as thoughts and emotions). The stronger the focus you bring to the task, the more likely you are to enter into a state of flow.

The increased creativity and focus that come with the state of flow lead to increased achievements. Knowing this can give you a new approach to productivity. When you get stuck and are in need of creative solutions or ideas, rather than trying harder, pause and activate the state of flow, because in flow the productivity and the ideas will flow easily.

EXERCISE 9:
FLOW

Activating the state of flow is especially useful when you are in need of new ideas or solutions to problems.

STEP 1. Setting a clear goal: Think about a situation that is causing you stress. Then finish this sentence with a clear goal for improving the situation and write it down.

How do I .../How can I ...

For example: How do I generate more revenue? How can I keep my toddler calm in the supermarket? How can I make more time to exercise?

STEP 2. Activating green brain: Focus on your breath. Notice what it feels like to breathe in and out. Do this without giving your opinion or wanting to change anything. Simply observe your breath and notice what happens in your body as you breathe in and out.

STEP 3. Combining green brain with clear goal for activation of flow: When you feel calm, focus on the question or desired outcome you have written down and write down whatever comes to your mind. When doing this make sure your hand keeps moving. Do not stop and think, just write down whatever comes to mind. Allow the thoughts and ideas to flow freely by not interrupting or judging them. When you begin to judge or evaluate your ideas, gently and kindly bring your attention back to your breath and the original question or goal.

STEP 4. When you feel as if you are running out of ideas, make yourself continue for at least three more minutes!

STEP 5. Once you have enough ideas, put down your pen. Now it is time to use your analyzing skills to see which ideas are useful.

Tip: *Coming up with ideas to reach a positive goal is easier for your brain than coming up with ideas to avoid something negative. For example:*

'How can my partner and I become closer?' works better than 'How can we stop arguing?'

Keep your goals positive and you will be surprised at the ideas you will come up with.

Overcoming blockages to flow

The most common blockages to entering or remaining in a state of flow are:

» Trying

» Imbalance between skills and challenges

» Negative thoughts and feelings

Trying

Flow happens in the green-brain state. When you are trying or striving, however, you activate the orange — achieving — brain state. There is nothing wrong with this, but it is not the optimal brain state for creative, high-level thinking. In the brain state of achieving you experience immediate thinking: your brain will scan your memory to look for knowledge and past events that were similar, and come up with ideas that are not new but instead familiar and obvious.

Imbalance between skills and challenges

A good balance between the task and your skills is helpful when it comes to reaching a state of flow. As Csíkszentmihályi describes, a task cannot be too easy, nor should it be too difficult.

If you are struggling to reach a state of flow, think about the diagram below and where you find yourself. Then ask yourself the question: Is there anything I can adjust or change to move closer to the flow channel?

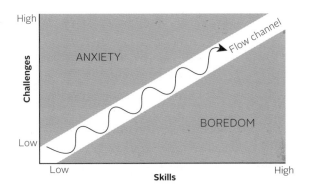

Negative thoughts and feelings

Negative thoughts tend to block the state of flow. Not only do they pose a distraction, your negative thoughts trigger the sequence of negative feelings that block flow.

Thoughts like:

I'm/my work is not good enough.

Others will judge me/my work.

I don't have enough time/support/resources/talent.

These thoughts immediately change your position on the flow chart and place you in the anxiety domain. This will, without exception, activate stress. To combat this, use Byron Katie's self-enquiry technique (see page 141) to turn these thoughts around. Or you can use the Acknowledge–Link–Let Go (ALL) model of processing emotions (see page 70) to process the negative emotions. These techniques help bring your brain back to the green brain from where you can reactivate the state of flow.

EXERCISE 10:
PRODUCTIVITY, CREATIVE THINKING AND SUCCESS

STEP 1. Activate green brain by using one of your personal green-brain activators or a green-brain exercise such as mindfulness or gratitude (see below).

STEP 2. Mindfully focus on your goal and progress so far, noticing it with kindness and without judgment.

STEP 3. Ask yourself, *What has worked well for me?* and write it down.

_____

_____

STEP 4. Then ask yourself, *How can I expand that/do more of that?* Notice what comes to mind and write it down.

_____

_____

STEP 5. Turn your focus back to your work and progress so far and ask yourself, *What is my number-one challenge?*

_____

_____

STEP 6. Notice what comes to mind with kindness and without judgment and ask yourself, *What would help?* Mindfully notice what comes to mind and write it down.

_____

_____

INCREASING PRESENT-MOMENT HAPPINESS THROUGH GRATITUDE

Finish this sentence: *I am so happy and grateful that ...*

_____

_____

_____

_____

_____

RENEW YOUR MIND TIP

When you are working on something and you feel stressed, remind yourself that if you 'take 5' you 'win 50'. In other words, if you take 5 minutes to activate flow, you will save at least 50 minutes on the total time you spend on this task.

CHAPTER 10:

The beginner's mind

One of the key elements of mindfulness is the beginner's mind. The beginner's mind is one of openness and curiosity without preconceived ideas and concepts. In a way, it is learning to approach and see things like a child again. This may sound strange because our society and educational system is focused on moving us away from the beginner's mind and making us experts in various areas. Being a beginner is not often seen as something valuable but rather as something unworthy and uncomfortable that we need to change.

I see the beginner's mind as a powerful tool, a way to achieve a calm, open and neutral way of thinking. The beginner's mind is also a technique to activate the green-brain state in challenging situations and see the situation from a mindful perspective rather than through your unhelpful glasses (your preconceived ideas and concepts that make you think and feel in a certain way). Approaching a challenging situation with a beginner's mind creates space for intuition, awareness and seeing things in a new light rather than automatically boxing it in.

To use the beginner's mind all you have to do is focus on a situation either in the moment or by thinking back to it later on. Try to focus on the situation as if you are seeing it for the very first time, as if you have no prior knowledge or opinions about anything or anyone in the situation. Instead you take on an open-minded, curious and non-judgmental attitude as you observe the situation.

For some people, it helps if they imagine they are a Martian who has just landed and is seeing this situation for the very first time. As a Martian, all you have are your senses to observe the situation. Then, in a kind and non-judgmental way, describe to yourself what you observe, only sticking to the facts. No mind-reading, no interpreting, no feeling-based judgments; simply state that facts of what is going on in front of you.

The beginner's mind technique helps you take a more neutral stance by making you 'step back' and observe the situation while focusing only on the facts. This helps you to stay in green brain and see things more clearly and accurately. The result is often a fresh, new and more helpful perspective.

The brain

Your brain is divided into three main areas. The first one is the brain stem. This is where our most basic life functions are located, such as breathing, heart rate and alertness. This part of the brain is often called the reptilian brain because it holds the functions we can also observe in reptiles.

The second area is called the limbic area. Among other things, this part of the brain is responsible for motivation, emotions, the attribution of meaning, memory and attachment.

The third area of the brain is known as the neocortex. This is an integrative area that ties together the social, the somatic and the analytical. The neocortex is the part of the brain that gives the ability for high-level thinking and analyzing.

The neocortex

The neocortex consists of six layers.

Bottom-up processing

The neocortex can be activated from the bottom up, starting at layer 6, then moving through layer 5, then 4, etc. This is called bottom-up processing.

When you have an experience for the first time you are more likely to use bottom-up processing. Remember when you drove a car for the first time? It is likely you remember this as being an intense and lively experience of the senses. Or think back to your first time on a plane, your first day at a new school, the first time you went on a date with the person who became your partner. Most people remember these occasions as 'feeling' moments. Even thinking back to them can trigger a sensory and emotional experience. It is likely that these were bottom-up experiences because you were experiencing them for the first time and there was no top-level concept created yet. You came into the situation as a beginner, without a 'cognitive box' to put it in.

This open, sensory, curious, not-knowing-what-will-happen-next way of experiencing things comes with your full attention and creates an intense sense of being present.

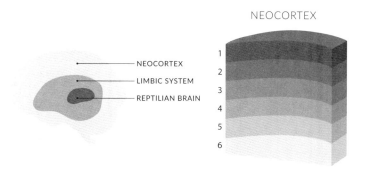

Top-down processing

Your brain also has the ability to activate the neocortex from the top down, starting at layer 1, then layer 2, then 3, etc. This is called top-down processing. When you have done something repeatedly your mind creates a top-down constraint to understand and store the information. You could say your brain becomes a bit lazy. Instead of taking in everything, your mind ticks the box of what it thinks is happening and goes with that information. This saves the brain energy and is an effective way of processing, leaving more energy and attention for other things.

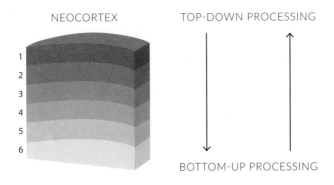

For example, when you now think about driving your car, you probably see it as just another thing you do. It won't trigger an intense 'feeling' experience like it did the very first time you drove your car. After a few months of driving, you can drive your car on autopilot. Then only the top levels of the neocortex are activated. This requires limited attention and focus, because your brain knows what is happening and what to expect.

When you think about your partner after you have been together for a number of years, you are less likely to have the intense experience you had when you first met. Your brain will simply 'activate' the box with this person's name on it and the concept you have constructed over the years.

Box thinking

In most cases the top-down processing system — or box thinking — is very useful. If everything you did or thought about required your full attention and activated a flood of sensory stimuli, you would not get much done. However, doing things on autopilot and simply activating a 'cognitive box' skews the reality. This happens in several ways.

Selective attention

One way your brain preserves the cognitive boxes is by selective attention. The mind is looking for information it is expecting to see. In other words, if you expect to see something, it is very likely that you will see that very thing. Your brain looks for 'evidence' that confirms your cognitive box and ignores information that does not fit into the box.

A study by the University of Hertfordshire showed that people who believed they were generally lucky were more likely to see the £5 note that had been placed on the floor by the researchers. Afterwards the people who believed they were lucky reported thoughts such as 'Wow, lucky me!', which confirmed and reinforced their pre-existing belief. The people who believed they were unlucky mostly stepped over the money without noticing it.

Bending the facts

Another way the mind conserves its cognitive boxes is by bending the facts. At a subconscious level, the mind reconstructs information to fit into the box. It does this because perceiving information that does not fit the box would require energy-costing processes to create another cognitive box or to change the existing cognitive box. This is an inefficient process that requires full attention and focus. Because the brain is programmed to save energy, it 'makes' the perceived information fit into the existing box.

Attributing

The third way in which the mind keeps its cognitive boxes intact is through attributing. When information is perceived that fits the box it will be attributed to the person involved and will be seen as part of their personality. When information is perceived that does not fit the box, the mind attributes it to circumstances or labels it as an exception.

For example, you are convinced your partner does not care about you and you have put them in the 'they do not care enough about me' box. Your mind will seek ways to confirm this as the truth.

1. Selective attention

» Whenever you are with them you will be paying attention to everything they do wrong (in your eyes). Your mind will not register the times they are caring and considerate.

2. Bending the facts

» When you notice your partner doing something caring you are likely to dismiss it as unimportant.

3. Attribution

» When your partner does something nice or caring you might think they are doing it for the wrong reasons. Or you will try to make circumstances — rather than your partner — responsible for the positive behaviour.

So, no matter the facts of the situation, your mind tries to keep your cognitive boxes intact, just to prevent having to switch to the energy-consuming bottom-up processing. When the preconceived ideas are positive this does not lead to problems. When the preconceived ideas are negative it leads to ongoing negative thoughts and feelings and stress.

The beginner's mind is a way to break free from unhelpful top-down constraints or boxes and make the mind apply bottom-up processing again. When you apply bottom-up processing the traps of selective attention, bending the facts and attribution are dealt with, which will result in a quick reduction of stress plus a new perspective on the situation.

EXERCISE 11:
BEGINNER'S MIND

STEP 1. For a moment, pretend you are from the planet Mars. Take an object — something you use in regular life — and observe it in an open, curious and non-judgmental way, as if you have never seen it before. Try to figure out what it is. Notice the colour, the shape, the details. Use your touch and smell to explore and observe the object.

STEP 2. Did you notice anything different or new when you were observing the object in this way?

STEP 3. Now focus on a situation that causes you stress or triggers a negative emotional response. Apply the beginner's mind to this situation by observing the facts in an open, curious and non-judgmental way, as if you were experiencing it for the first time. It might help if you imagine once again you are from the planet Mars. What do you hear and see? Try to leave your own thoughts and feelings out of the observation. If they pop up, simply notice this and in a kind and non-judgmental way turn your attention back to the situation.

STEP 4. What are you becoming aware of now?

_____

_____

_____

_____

_____

_____

_____

_____

How to apply the beginner's mind in daily life

Regular practice of the beginner's mind will make it easier for your brain to access bottom-up processing. Your brain literally strengthens the bottom-up pathways every time you use them.

You can practise the beginner's mind any time, anywhere. An effective way to practise is to use the beginner's mind whenever you are feeling stressed, frustrated or any other negative emotion. You can use it in the moment or afterwards by focusing on the facts of the situation, without engaging your opinions and preconceived ideas. Using the Martian concept can make it easier but it is not necessary. When you apply the beginner's mind in a moment of stress you will find your stress levels drop and your brain moves towards the green part of the spectrum, which opens up the way to creative thinking, problem-solving and open communication.

When your brain has been hijacked by stress and you have responded in a way that you regret or that just was not effective, it can still pay off to use the beginner's mind. Take a moment to think of the situation and apply the beginner's mind; then, when you are observing the facts of what has happened, you can ask yourself the question: 'How do I want to respond?'

For example, one of my clients works for a large humanitarian aid organization. She had an overloaded work schedule and completely missed the information that on a particular day she was supposed to deliver a speech regarding a new children's project. Normally she would have felt overwhelmed and self-critical, and the stress resulting from her lack of preparation would have hijacked her brain, making her unable to clearly articulate her ideas. She decided to try the beginner's mind. When she looked only at the facts, she saw a room full of people who were all passionate about making this project a success. No one was there to judge her or criticize her; they were all there to make a difference in the lives of underprivileged children. Focusing on these facts, rather than on herself and her lack of preparation, allowed her to move away from the red brain and into the green brain. It reduced her stress and, instead of literally wanting to run away and hide, she became excited about being part of this group of people. She was able to convey her message, and her involvement in the project became a great success.

When it doesn't work

Like most mind-training techniques, the hardest part is to make a conscious effort to put it into practice. At some level we like our glasses and our boxes, and letting go of them can seem very unfair and wrong, and sometimes leaves us feeling very vulnerable. Applying the beginner's mind is hardest when you are angry with someone, or a situation has hurt you, but in those situations it can be most effective.

When you are faced with internal resistance, I recommend that you respond in a kind and non-judgmental way. One way to mindfully connect with your resistance is by using Acknowledge–Link–Let Go. Often your resistance will lessen. Hopefully you will begin to see that the only one who is suffering from holding on to this 'box thinking' is you, and that you owe it to yourself to become unstuck from it.

If this process does not happen, don't judge it but continue to meet your resistance with kindness and acceptance. Self-compassion is the fastest way to the green brain.

 ## RENEW YOUR MIND TIP

Try the beginner's mind when you need new ideas or solutions at work. It helps you think 'out of the box' and come up with new, creative ideas.

CHAPTER 11:

Improving relationships

Happiness is a phenomenon on which countless studies have been conducted. One of the clearest findings to emerge from research on happiness is that we are social creatures and a lack of good social relationships damages our health and our happiness. It turns out that not having close relationships poses the same risk to your health as smoking and obesity.

Relationships include romantic relationships, relationships with family members, friends, neighbours, colleagues and anyone we feel connected to. Both the quality and the quantity of our relationships impact our health, longevity and psychological wellbeing. Having a network of social connections or a few close relationships increases immune-system function and helps protect us from cardiovascular disease and age-related mental decline.

Mindful connection

Mindful connection is a bottom-up 'feeling experience' that occurs when two brains in the green-brain state interact. Mindful connection can be a deep and rewarding experience, the kind that strengthens your bond and makes you feel loved, supported, understood and valued. It is sometimes described as 'heart to heart' connection.

In mindful connection, the lower levels of the cortex and the subcortical regions of the brain are activated. This is responsible for giving you a 'feeling experience' that your brain interprets as meaningful. Rapid neural signal transfer takes place and the chemical oxytocin (among others) is released, leading to softened facial muscles and tone of voice and an increased openness of the perceptual system.

How to achieve mindful connection

Just like general mindfulness, mindful connection has the following two components.

» **Attention** — paying attention to both the person we are connecting with and what they are sharing with us.

» **Attitude** — paying attention in a kind, non-judgmental way.

We can focus our attention in different ways, and how we focus our attention determines if the interaction will be mindful or unmindful. Mindfully paying attention means focusing on the person and their message and fighting outward distractions. This sounds simple but in reality it can be very hard. Often, we are not actually paying attention when talking to others; instead we are looking at our phone, the TV, cooking dinner or tidying up. It is possible to listen when you are doing something else, but as soon as you do more than one thing at a time you are multitasking. When you multitask, your brain seeks ways to minimize the energy spent on each task, and activating top-down processing is one of the brain's first go-to ways to preserve energy. As we discussed in the previous chapter, top-down processing causes boxed-in thinking and activation of preconceived ideas and opinions. The more distractions, the more top-down processing and the more difficult it becomes to connect mindfully.

There is a time and place for multitasking, but it is not when you want to mindfully connect with someone. Mindful connection starts with giving your undivided attention to both the person and what they are sharing with you. This doesn't mean you have to sit still and look each other in the eyes (even though that is a great exercise to increase mindful connection). You can be doing other things as long as your main focus is on the person you are connecting with.

> In order to have mindful connection you need to fight *external* distractions — disconnect to connect.

In order to connect mindfully we also need to fight internal distractions. Your thoughts, opinions, judgments and feelings can form distractions that stop you from simply connecting and listening to the other person. So often we are listening not to understand but to answer. Mindful connection starts with being available mentally — creating the mental space to listen to the other person in an open, curious and non-judgmental way first before we respond.

> In order to have mindful connection you need to fight *internal* distractions — notice them and let go.

This brings us to the second element of mindful connection: attitude. In other words, how do you treat the information that is being shared with you? Mindful connection comes from accepting the other person's thoughts and feelings and staying out of judgment. It is listening with the aim to understand, not with the aim to reply. Your opinions and judgments come up automatically and it is therefore hard to not be distracted by them, but with practice you can learn to let them go and listen without being distracted by your opinions or thoughts.

Professor Daniel Siegel sums it up beautifully in his definition of mindful connection or, as he calls it, attunement.

> 'Attunement is how we focus our attention on others and take their essence into our world.'

INSIGHT INSPIRATION

1. Who are the most important people in your life?

   _____

   _____

2. What *external* distractions get in the way of mindfully connecting with them (for example, your phone, TV or housework)?

   _____

   _____

3. What *internal* distractions get in the way of mindfully connecting with them (for example, worries about work, tiredness, judgments)?

   _____

   _____

4. What changes are you willing to make to ensure fewer distractions and more moments of mindful connection with these important people?

   _____

   _____

   _____

RENEW YOUR MIND TIP

Practise your listening skills by starting a conversation with a question. Try to listen to the answer with the aim of understanding the person and their experience, without adding anything to it.

Oxytocin

Also known as the 'love hormone' or 'cuddle hormone', oxytocin is not the only chemical responsible for mindful connection but it does play a crucial role in social connection and activation of the green brain. This hormone has many beneficial effects, including the following.

» Increases energy

» Fights depressive symptoms

» Promotes social behaviour and bonding

» Makes us better at picking up and understanding social cues

» Lowers stress and anxiety (by lowering cortisol and adrenaline levels)

» Makes learning more effective

» Makes you more trusting

» Makes you more trustworthy

» Makes you more generous

'Oxytocin solidifies the glue that binds us into meaningful and important relationships.'

— *Sara Algoe*

Oxytocin plays a key role in mindful connection. The more often your brain produces oxytocin the easier it becomes for the brain to produce it. Oxytocin can't be purchased in a pharmacy, but luckily research shows you can boost your oxytocin levels naturally with the following steps.

1. Eye contact

One of the reasons couples who are in love gaze into each other's eyes is because of high oxytocin levels. Research shows that prolonged eye contact is not only a result of high oxytocin, it can also be a way to raise oxytocin.

Most people avoid looking in another's eyes for a long time; instead they glance over people. You can be around people all day without really making eye contact. To change this, make a conscious effort to look people in the eye. It might feel strange and unnatural in the beginning, but you will feel more connected to others and they will feel more connected to you. There is something open and genuine about having someone really look you in the eye when they are talking to you. It literally makes you feel seen.

2. Touch

Touch is another way to naturally raise oxytocin levels. A hug, a handshake, putting your hand on someone's shoulder. People with high oxytocin levels are more likely to touch others but it also works the other way around; making a conscious effort to (appropriately) touch others will increase oxytocin levels in both you and the other person. It will make them feel touched in the positive sense of the word.

Some examples from studies include: when a teacher touches a student gently on their back or shoulder, the student is more likely to participate in class; athletes who high-five or hug their teammates perform better in team sport; a friendly touch can make patients like their doctors more; when faced with a stressful situation, participants who were holding hands or being hugged showed lower levels of stress than those who were not.

 ## RENEW YOUR MIND TIP

Create micro-moments of mindful connection with your family by making a conscious effort to make real eye contact and touch them. It will help you be present and make you feel more connected to them and them feel more connected to you.

3. Physical exercise

Exercise is healthy in many ways. One surprising benefit of physical exercise is that it raises oxytocin levels. Studies have been conducted on people running, walking outside and playing team sports, and all of these activities are effective in boosting oxytocin.

We all know that exercise is healthy, but not many people know that it also works as a powerful antidepressant. Various studies show that exercise works better than antidepressant medication in preventing relapse into depression. A study by Dr Blumenthal showed that 10 months of regular, moderate exercise outperformed a leading antidepressant (Zoloft) in easing depressive symptoms in young adults. Another study found that walking for 20–30 minutes per day reduced depressive symptoms faster than antidepressant medication. In another study, one group of participants was given both antidepressant medication and an exercise program. The results showed that physical exercise was the more effective depression fighter.

 RENEW YOUR MIND TIP

Parking a block away from your destination, taking the stairs instead of the elevator, having walking meetings — these are all simple ways to increase both your health and your mood.

4. Giving

Studies show that artificially increasing oxytocin levels makes people more generous. Again, this also works the other way around: by giving a gift, no matter how small, you will boost your oxytocin and that of the person who receives the gift.

By giving a friend a cup of tea, buying a colleague lunch, donating to charity, shouting yourself a gift, even by giving way to a stranger you are raising oxytocin levels in yourself and the other person. This creates a micro-moment of connection and makes the other person feel valued.

When it comes to oxytocin, a reward does not achieve the same effect as a gift. A gift that is not linked to achievement but is purely to appreciate a person or a moment is the more powerful oxytocin booster. Such a gift makes people feel loved and appreciated for who they are, not for what they do.

5. Petting an animal

Research shows that petting an animal raises oxytocin levels quickly. People can have incredibly strong bonds with their pets. Oxytocin plays a key role in creating this bond. Petting an animal has a strong stress-reducing, calming effect on both the person and the pet. Animal-aided therapies are hence very effective in increasing connection, health and wellbeing in patients. Petting an animal is even linked to improvement in social skills. Studies show that regular interaction with animals is beneficial for children with autism and the elderly who suffer from depression and loneliness.

6. Sex

Sex stimulates the production of oxytocin in both men and women. Again, this relationship works both ways: having high oxytocin levels will make you feel more connected and more interested in having sex, and having sex will make you feel more connected due to the rise in oxytocin.

Sex is an important part of mindful connection with your partner. When life gets busy it is not always easy to maintain a good sex life or even to maintain intimacy and connection with your partner. Often partners become like colleagues who are running a project together called family. Or partners are so caught up in work that they don't make time to connect with each other. For many busy people sex is just not a priority, but not prioritizing sex has consequences, one of which is that it takes away from mindful connection and opens up the way for irritations and disconnection.

It may feel counterintuitive but prioritizing intimacy including sex, especially when you are not getting along, does make sense. It boosts oxytocin levels and will help you to reconnect.

7. Gratitude

Expressing gratitude, whether it is out loud or internal, raises oxytocin levels. In one study, remembering something nice a partner had done made the participants' oxytocin levels rise and made them feel more loving, peaceful and connected to their partner. A similar study, in which participants were asked to remember or share a positive experience, resulted in a similar rise in positive emotions but no rise in oxytocin. There seems to be something specific about gratitude that activates the oxytocin system in the brain. Perhaps it is because gratitude brings awareness to our co-dependence and the importance of our relationships.

EXERCISE 12:
IMPROVING RELATIONSHIPS

STEP 1. Think about an important person in your life.

STEP 2. See this person in front of you, their whole body or just their face. Picture them, as if they were right there. What is it about them that you love? What things about their personality do you appreciate? What do they do for you that you can be grateful for?

_____

_____

_____

STEP 3. Is there anyone else in your life that you can be grateful for? Picture that person. What is it about them that you like? What do they do for you that you can be grateful for?

_____

_____

_____

RENEW YOUR MIND TIP

If there is tension or irritation in your relationship, dedicate yourself to one week of daily practice of this exercise. Take a moment each day to think of something you appreciate about your partner and write this down. You will notice this helps you see your partner in a more positive light, which opens the way to reconnecting.

CHAPTER 12:

Solutions for conflict

Not many things are as stressful as conflict with an important person in your life. Even conflict with someone who is not important to you can cause high levels of stress. From an evolutionary point of view it makes a lot of sense: in ancient times not only our wellbeing but also our survival depended on relationships and our position within a group. Being in conflict could lead to losing the protection and therefore safety of the group. This is why alarm bells go off in your brain when conflict arises. That uneasy, uncomfortable or stressful feeling that comes with having a conflict is your brain telling you, 'It's not safe!' Yet conflict, especially conflict with those closest to us, is part of life. Everyone encounters conflict at some stage: conflict with your partner, your mother, a friend or conflict with a colleague or a boss.

Conflict begins with the activation of the red-brain state in at least one of the people involved.

The red-brain state is activated when a person *perceives* a threat, be it physical, emotional or social. When you feel offended or mistreated the red brain can kick into gear, which leads to several things. Adrenaline is released within seconds and cortisol is released within minutes. The red-brain dynamics have been described in previous chapters but let me refresh your memory with a list of things that occur when your brain is in the red zone.

Physical effects:

» Tunnel vision

» Shallow breathing

» Stopped or slowed digestion

» Increased blood pressure and blood sugar

» Increased heart rate

» Suppressed immune system

» Tensed muscles

Psychological effects:

» Judgmental and black-and-white thinking

» Feeling stressed

» Narrow or fixed point of view

» Unkind manner

» Disconnection from others

In the case of a physical threat, the stress response will help you to survive: it makes you run faster, fight better, stay completely focused, make quick decisions and respond swiftly to fight off the threat. In case of an emotional or social threat, however, activation of the red brain is not helpful at all. The red-brain state blocks you from thinking clearly and objectively. It stops you from seeing the bigger picture and the other person's intention. Instead, your mind takes shortcuts and projects your stressful thoughts onto the situation (usually without realizing it). The red brain makes you impulsive and either suppresses emotions or becomes stuck in them. It blocks effective communication, empathy and connection, which can lead to withdrawing or overreaction and conflict.

It is not difficult to see how these psychological effects can quickly lead to responses that are then perceived as a threat by the other person. This will then trigger the red-brain state in them as well. When two brains in the red-brain state interact, the opposite of mindful connection happens — conflict.

Two brains in the red zone are both perceiving their own reality, which is based on their glasses. They quickly lose connection and because their brain feels threatened they will respond with defence, freeze or attack. It is important to keep in mind that this might not always be visible on the outside; emotionally withdrawing or suppressing anger can be a result of conflict too.

Take the following dialogue between a husband and wife, for example. They both start off with a neutral, green-brain state.

Jane comes home from shopping and takes a loaf of bread out of the bag.

Mark: 'We don't need bread. Didn't you check in the cupboard before you went shopping?'

Looking at the facts, this question is neutral. It could even be seen as very useful advice, to check the cupboard before going shopping. However, it could be interpreted in several ways. Let's say Jane experiences it as criticism. She then perceives a threat, which activates her red brain.

She feels a knot in her stomach, her heart rate goes up and her breathing becomes shallow. Her thinking becomes judgmental and black-and-white: *He always does this, he always criticizes me and questions everything I do!*

Because her mind feels unsafe it responds with: *He should just mind his own business and stop judging me.* These thoughts make her feel both sad and angry and she responds by impulsively reacting in an unkind way: 'If you're so perfect, then why don't you do the shopping from now on!'

This response is interpreted by Mark as rude, angry and unfair. Therefore his brain *perceives* it as an emotional and personal attack, which activates the red brain in him as well.

Mark feels tension in his neck and shoulder area, his heart rate goes up and his breathing becomes shallow. His thinking becomes judgmental and black-and-white — *No matter what I say I never do it right, she's never satisfied and always finds something to complain about.* Because his mind feels unsafe and under attack, it responds with defence. *She should stop being so bloody moody and stop criticizing everything!* These thoughts make him feel offended and annoyed and he responds impulsively by walking away in angry silence. The consequence is disconnection, no further communication, and both Jane and Mark feel hurt and angry and blame the other person for causing the problem.

Stressful thoughts and core beliefs

Rather than approaching each situation based on its facts, the red brain makes you refer back to old patterns — including recurring stressful thoughts and negative core beliefs — which are well-rehearsed neural pathways. Your brain then 'projects' these thoughts and core beliefs onto the situation and looks for 'evidence' that this projection is indeed true. To the person in the red-brain state it feels like they are seeing the facts, when in reality they are seeing a projection of their own thoughts and feelings. Most often people simply assume they are seeing the truth and never question what they think they see. This can easily lead to misunderstandings and conflicts. Here is an example.

James

Recurring stressful thought: *I will make a mistake.*

Red-brain core belief: *I am a failure and others will reject me.*

'*Charlotte is giving me a to-do list because she thinks I will be sitting around doing nothing all day. She even calls to check in on what I'm doing. She must think I'm wasting my time.*'

Charlotte

Recurring stressful thought: *Others need me.*

Red-brain core belief: *I need to be caring and supportive in order not to lose people's love.*

'*James is going through a difficult time with the redundancy. He needs my support but I have to finish my work. I have to help him fill his days and be in touch or else he will think that I don't care.*'

It is not hard to see how believing your projection can lead to disconnection and conflict. In the short term it can cause miscommunication and conflict, and in the long term damaged or broken relationships.

Drama Triangle

Two red brains interacting can easily lead to conflict. The Drama Triangle is a helpful tool in understanding the dynamics of conflict and the role you play in it. A psychological and social model of conflict first described by Stephen Karpman in 1968, it describes three common roles people can take on in conflict.

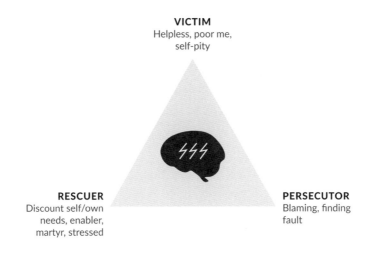

VICTIM
Helpless, poor me,
self-pity

RESCUER
Discount self/own
needs, enabler,
martyr, stressed

PERSECUTOR
Blaming, finding
fault

Victim

The main emotions of the victim are those of sadness and fear. The victim is unable to stand up for themselves and tends to avoid confrontation. In conflict the victim feels hurt, helpless and incapable. They then feel sorry for themselves and dwell on this feeling without taking any appropriate action to change the situation. The victim feels stuck in victimhood and blames their lack of skills or resources on others. This can lead to passive–aggressive behaviour and giving in to unhelpful things in order to feel better. In this role, the victim does not take responsibility for their own feelings or actions.

Common core belief: *I can't do it by myself/There is something wrong with me.*

Mantra: *I need others.*

Underlying need: *To be rescued.*

Underlying motivation: *If you take care of me I can be okay.*

For example, Matt always has problems. He suffers from health issues, struggles at work, and finds it difficult to manage all his responsibilities at home and his finances. There is always a problem — so it seems. When solutions are suggested his response is, 'Yes, but . . .' Because of the strong belief that he is incapable, he constantly feels inadequate. This leads to a strong dependency on others and constant worries about potential future problems.

Persecutor

The main emotion of the persecutor is that of frustration/ anger (underlying is fear). In conflict, the persecutor finds fault in others and blames others. They feel angry, frustrated and entitled, and are likely to use anger and criticism. The persecutor is often verbally strong and attacks when venting in order to release stress. They have a strong sense of justice. This combined with feeling under attack leads to hurtful behaviours that are then justified by the persecutor. They focus on other people's faults to avoid having to take responsibility for their own and make changes.

Common core belief: *Others are mean/out to get me.*

Mantra: *It's your fault.*

Underlying need: *To be in control.*

Underlying motivation: *As long as I am in control you can't hurt me.*

For example, Diana has a strong presence. She can be charming and caring, or defensive and intimidating and lash out verbally. The sharpness of her tongue and the unpredictability of her moods make others feel uncomfortable. When issues arise she always has to be right and will find clever answers and reasons as to why she is. This makes people pull away. When this happens she feels abandoned and confirmed in her belief that people can't be trusted and she can only rely on herself.

Rescuer

The main emotions for the rescuer are anxiety and guilt. In order to avoid feeling anxious or guilty, the rescuer comes to the rescue of others. They discount their own needs and focus on the needs of others. This may seem selfless and altruistic but this behaviour serves a self-centred purpose: to reduce the rescuer's own anxiety and make them feel responsible and good about themselves. By their actions they make themselves a martyr who feels overstretched and makes unhealthy sacrifices and sets bad priorities. They do not take responsibility for their own needs and rob others of the responsibility to take care of theirs. Rescuers might end up not only sacrificing their own needs to rescue others but they may also sacrifice the needs of those closest to them.

Common core belief: *I am responsible for others.*

Mantra: *I will fix it.*

Underlying need: *To be needed.*

Underlying motivation: *If you need me you won't leave me.*

For example, Katie suffers from adrenal fatigue and has spent many years in an unhealthy relationship. For years she believed her partner would change, and even in the face of clear signs that he wouldn't, she kept fixing things for him in the hope things would get better. She is a 'yes' person and over-commits because she feels it is her responsibility to help others where she can. In her over-committing she is failing to take care of her own health, her wellbeing and that of her three children.

There is usually one role in which we tend to enter the Drama Triangle. This role is also called our 'starting gate' and is tied to our core beliefs about others, the world and ourselves. After entering the Drama Triangle we can move between the different roles. Sometimes we tend to take on a specific role within a specific relationship or situation. At other times we shift roles within one conversation. The move from one role to another can happen very quickly and we can even move back and forth between roles in a matter of minutes.

'The Victim is not really as helpless as he feels, the Rescuer is not really helping and the Persecutor does not really have a valid complaint.'

— *Claude Steiner*

A way out

No one in the Drama Triangle wins; it is a lose–lose situation, but there is a way out of this negative red-brain triangle of conflict and disconnect. Disagreements, conflicts of interest and arguments are part of life. You are not able to control all of your circumstances or other people's behaviours but you can control your own brain state, even when you are in a conflict or disagreement. When you keep your own brain in the green zone, the dynamics of the conflict will change drastically and you will have better outcomes.

Solution Triangle

The green-brain or mindful version of conflict is represented in the Solution Triangle. The Solution Triangle is a more helpful alternative to the Drama Triangle and is based on the 'Winner's Triangle' proposed by Acey Choy in 1990.

VULNERABLE
Awareness without
judgment, openness

CARING
Compassion, supporting
without taking over
responsibility

ASSERTIVE
Taking healthy
actions, setting
clear boundaries

Vulnerable

Being vulnerable is the helpful version of being a victim. Vulnerability has two layers. First, it means being vulnerable and open towards yourself. Rather than suppressing thoughts and feelings, you mindfully allow them to be there even if they are not pretty or comfortable. One way of doing this is by using Acknowledge–Link–Let Go, the mindfulness tool for processing emotions (see page 70). When you are vulnerable and accept your emotions, instead of taking over, your feelings become like a compass that you can use to figure out what is being triggered for you and what need is not being met. This insight can then be used to figure out appropriate solutions and ways forward. The key combination to being vulnerable is accepting your thoughts and feelings without discounting your skills and abilities to problem-solve.

For example, Jim's colleague fails to give him the information he needs to do his work. He feels frustrated and ignored and is in victim mode. He uses Acknowledge–Link–Let Go to process his feelings. When he thinks about the situation with a calm mind he sees that his colleague is not making his job hard on purpose. He is under a lot of pressure and is unable to handle his caseload. It is nothing personal.

The second layer of being vulnerable is sharing your thoughts and feelings with the person with whom you are in conflict, giving them insight into how you feel in a way that does not attack them or take over their responsibility. This position is called 'vulnerable' for a reason. Being vulnerable in conflict is not easy — it might feel uncomfortable or even unsafe — but it is very powerful.

A very effective way to give the other person insight into your thoughts and feelings is to use this technique:

'When you ... It makes me feel/I feel ...'

This approach helps you describe your experience of the situation in a way that is unlikely to raise resistance.

For example, Rachael's partner had been complaining all week about being tired and asked to postpone their date night because he did not have the energy to go out. Yet when his friends phoned him the following day and invited him to the football he accepted and stayed out until 2 a.m. This left Rachael feeling angry and unloved. When she applied Acknowledge–Link–Let Go she tapped into the underlying hurt and sadness that was coming from a feeling of being rejected. Instead of feeling sorry for herself or giving her partner the silent treatment she chose to be vulnerable. She waited until the next day and told him:

'It really hurts me that you don't have the energy to go out with me but you can go out until 2 a.m. with your friends. It makes me feel rejected and as if you don't care about me.'

Her partner acknowledged that this was not fair and suggested he would take her out for dinner that evening.

Assertive

Being assertive is the green-brain version of being a persecutor. When you are assertive you are taking healthy actions that take care of your own unmet needs. You are not defending yourself but taking care of yourself. Assertiveness is something that follows from awareness and introspection. In order to understand what you really need, you first need to identify what you are really feeling underneath all the initial emotions of despair, anger or responsibility. Assertiveness begins with allowing yourself to pause and turn inwards. You can use Acknowledge–Link–Let Go for this and add to it the question: *How do I want to respond?*

Assertive actions are sometimes as simple as taking time for yourself because you realize you desperately need it, or saying no to requests because you need something else in that moment.

Following are some examples of what assertive actions can look like:

» Asking for what you want
» Saying no to what you don't want

» Giving feedback about behaviour that is causing a problem and being clear about what you would like to change

» Negotiating solutions that work for everyone

» Using your problem-solving skills to have your needs met, even when the other person does not change

For example, Jamie's sister invited him to come over for dinner to spend time with his young nephew. Jamie had a full-on day at work and wasn't able to leave the office on time to beat the traffic, and he knew he had another stressful day tomorrow. He became frustrated that his sister always invited him at the last minute. He felt frustrated and stuck. When he applied Acknowledge–Link–Let Go he identified that most of his stress came from feeling that he was not given a choice. In his mind, he had to go. After breathing out and letting it go he asked himself the question: What do I need? He identified that he needed some down time. Then he asked himself the question: How do I want to respond? He decided to call his sister and explain his situation and his decision to stay home that evening. To his surprise she was very understanding and not bothered at all.

Caring

Being caring is the green-brain version of rescuing. Being caring means being compassionate without taking over responsibility or ignoring your own needs. A key skill in caring is listening without trying to 'fix things'.

Following are some examples of what caring actions can look like:

» Invite others into problem-solving

» Be a mirror not a fixer; offer feedback on how you perceive the other person and their situation

» Give practical information that might help

Tip: If you tend to adopt the rescuer role, this trick can help you to stay in the caring role: keep your back against the chair — because as soon as you enter the rescuer mode your posture will become active instead of relaxed.

For example, Martha was asked to volunteer for a charity. She valued the organization and felt honoured, yet she felt it was not the right time for her to take on this role. She was aware of her rescuing tendencies and chose to be assertive instead. She knew, however, how desperate the director was and she mirrored and linked this in their conversation. This made the director feel supported and heard even though Martha declined the offer. Martha then suggested several people the director could approach for the role.

When you find yourself in a conflict, pause and think about your role. Are you in the role of victim, persecutor or rescuer? Once you have identified your position in the red-brain Drama Triangle, find the green-brain Solution Triangle version of your role and take the steps needed to move from your current role into the Solution Triangle role. You can also simply ask yourself, what would vulnerable (or transparent), assertive and caring action look like in this situation? This will change the dynamics of the situation and greatly increase the likelihood of a good outcome.

More techniques to help you be mindful in conflict

You can use mindfulness of the breath and mindfulness of the senses to help you back into the here and now and calm down. You can use Acknowledge–Link–Let Go to process the emotions you are feeling and come back to a green state. You can use self-enquiry to analyze the thoughts that are fuelling your red brain and turn them around to make your way back to the green zone. But there are more techniques available. Here are some of my favourite techniques for being mindful in conflict.

1. The beginner's mind

In conflict, 'box thinking' can kick in. Applying the beginner's mind helps keep your brain in the green zone or brings it back to the green zone. Then, from this calmer and clearer place you can decide how you want to respond.

2. Does it really matter?

It is often the small things — like a pair of socks left on the floor, the toothpaste cap off, a change of plans or an unanswered call — that become a reason for conflict. Sometimes we need to ask ourselves: Does it really matter? Taking a moment to consider the importance of things can help us stay in the green-brain zone and stop a way of thinking that will lead our brain into the red zone.

3. Focus on intention

One of the symptoms of the red brain is that we lose sight of the other person's intention because perspective-taking and empathy are blocked.

One way to keep your brain in the green zone — or bring it back — is to focus on the other person's intention. What is their intention? What are they trying to achieve? What is the goal or the need they are trying to fulfill?

4. Whose business is it?

As soon as you interfere with someone else's business or responsibility you will feel stressed because you have no control. Their behaviour is not your responsibility, but theirs; how you *respond* to their behaviour is your responsibility.

When you stay in the part that actually is your responsibility, you are more likely to maintain a green-brain state, which makes you better at managing your response. As soon as you move into someone else's responsibility — *they should do this, they shouldn't think this, it's not fair for them to feel this* — you are moving towards the red zone. This leads to stress, making it harder to manage your behaviour.

How to tie it all together

You can use one technique at a time, but combining them can increase the effect. For example:

One client's biggest frustration was the fact that her partner left his shoes at the door rather than putting them on the rack. She had raised this with him many times, but it didn't change. This made her feel hurt and angry.

She applied Acknowledge–Link–Let Go. This made her see that his action — or inaction — made her feel as if he did not care about her or her needs and ultimately that he did not love her. She had given the pair of shoes the label 'I don't care what you think because I don't love you'. When you attach this label to a pair of shoes it becomes much more than just a pair of shoes. Every time she saw the shoes next to the door this label made her feel hurt and rejected.

Then we used the self-enquiry technique. This made her realize that the shoes left at the door did not actually mean that her partner did not love her, and that he showed in many ways that he did indeed love her. It also made her realize that her approach to the shoe situation was far from loving towards him.

Then she used the beginner's mind and as she looked at the facts she could see a pair of shoes in the hallway and herself becoming really angry.

She asked herself the question: Does it really matter that his shoes are next to the door instead of on the rack? The answer was no, it doesn't really matter.

She continued by asking: What is his intention? Her answer was that there probably was no negative intention. He didn't leave the shoes at the door with the intention of annoying her.

And finally she asked herself: Whose business is it? She saw that her partner putting his shoes next to the rack was *his* business. Her response to this was *her* business, her responsibility. She had been so caught up with her own thoughts and feelings about his business that she had failed to take care of hers. Because of that she had become angry, frustrated and her behaviour was far from loving and kind.

After this she decided that every time she saw his shoes next to the rack she would remind herself that it did not matter and use a mantra that reminded her that her partner loved her.

All of these strategies are tools for your mindfulness-in-conflict tool kit. They are all slightly different ways to reach the same end goal: to keep your brain in the green zone or help bring you back to the green zone. Some tools may work for you, some may not — the only way to find out is to try them a couple of times. Then you will naturally stick with the ones that work best for you.

 RENEW YOUR MIND TIP

Try to catch irritations and frustration early on and apply the techniques when things don't feel like a big deal yet. Prevention of conflict is better than cure.

CHAPTER 13:

The purple brain and courage

The key to living everyday life from the green brain is not to eliminate all sources of stress (which would be impossible anyway). Instead, it starts with being able to discern 'primary stress' from 'secondary stress'. Secondary stress is all the stress that comes from the non-truths we tell ourselves, our overreacting, catastrophizing and needless worrying. Its impact and effects can range from annoying to debilitating, but no matter how strongly it impacts us, it is needless stress and a waste of energy, and can be eliminated through renewing your mind and changing your thoughts. By using mindfulness, focusing on your breath and senses, processing your emotions, using the self-enquiry technique and green-brain posture and facial expressions, you can learn to reduce stress and keep your brain in the green zone even when challenged by circumstances. For some people, mastering these techniques will eliminate as much as 99 per cent of the stress from their life.

Then you are left with the primary stress. These are substantial challenges you face, whether it's struggling to pay your bills, dealing with a manager who treats you unfairly or having to rush your child to the ER after a fall. In these situations, red brain (fight-or-flight) is understandable and makes perfect sense but isn't helpful, and because of the nature of the situation, trying to reduce the stress with the techniques above might not be effective. These situations are genuine emergencies, threats to your safety, your health, your loved ones, your career, your home, threats to your values, all the things that matter most to you. However, both history and the latest research on stress tell us that there is a powerful brain state that allows you to deal with high-stress situations without reverting to red brain self-defence. The alternative to red brain is the state of courage or, as I like to call it, purple brain.

Just think about a mama bear fearlessly fighting off a predator to protect her cubs, a man risking his own life by crawling out on the ice to save a dog who can't make it back to land on its own, a whistleblower outing a large corporation's evil actions at the risk of losing their own career and income. This state that drives us to self-sacrifice for a higher purpose instead of self-preservation (red brain) is purple brain.

When stress is inevitably high, purple-brain courage is the healthy alternative to red-brain fear or anger. Purple brain occurs when stress is high but so is the hope that your actions can make a difference. The word hope is important here because courage is mostly activated when the threat is perceived as strong and you are not sure you have what it takes to overcome it. It is the *hope*, not the *knowing*, that your actions can make a difference and a willingness to take that chance even if the cost is high that are the true markers of courage.

Fear	Anxiety	Calm assertive	Active assertive	Anger	Courage
Red brain	Orange brain	Green brain	Orange brain	Red brain	Purple brain
Strong threat	Low threat	No threat	Low threat	Medium threat	Strong threat
High stress	Medium stress	Low stress	Low–medium stress	Medium–high stress	High stress becomes reduced
External locus of control	External locus of control	Internal locus of control	Internal locus of control	Internal locus of control	Internal locus of control

Courage and the brain

Courage is a biologically engineered state that decreases fear and increases hope. It allows you to tolerate higher levels of risk and triggers a drive to action. To act courageously is to voluntarily act in a way that is the opposite of action promoted by fear. When you choose to act courageously, a part of the brain called the subgenual anterior cingulate cortex is activated. Oxytocin inhibits the activity of the amygdala, the fear centre of the brain, so we momentarily feel less fear and more empathy, connectedness and trust. In a state of courage, dopamine is also released further dampening the fear and increasing the motivation to act, preventing you from 'freezing'. Serotonin is also released, which impacts the attunement system thereby improving perception, intuition and self-control to ensure your actions will be executed skilfully and effectively. This cocktail of courage chemicals prevents you from succumbing to the fear-driven freeze or flight response and also prevents you from reverting to red-brain anger and aggression. Instead it drives you to altruistic, assertive and skilful action.

The courage or fear switch

Courage doesn't begin in the *absence* of fear; it begins *with* fear. When we experience fear our brain can choose one of two pathways. It can go down the fear pathway (red brain) or switch to the courage pathway (purple brain). This theory is supported by new research from the Stanford University School of Medicine that describes some fascinating insights into the brain in a state of courage. The researchers tested the response of mice in a threatening predator situation and measured their brain activity. They found that all of the mice responded to the threat with fear and would either freeze or flee. The researchers discovered that the brain area that becomes active when the mouse is experiencing fear is the xiphoid nucleus. This nucleus, which is located in the centre of the brain, is connected to the amygdala (threat detection), the prefrontal cortex (the thinking brain) and reward centres in the brain. When they artificially increased the activity in the xiphoid nucleus, the mice's behaviour changed drastically. When the part of the nucleus that connects to the amygdala (fear centre) was stimulated, the mice became more fearful and reacted by freezing or running away (red brain). When the part of the nucleus that connects to the cortex or thinking brain was stimulated, the mice would shift from fearful to courageous behaviour (purple brain). Instead of freezing or hiding, the mice started to rattle their tails, make a lot of noise and try to attack the predator.

It seems that the xiphoid nucleus works as a 'switch' between fear turning into red-brain limbic action or purple-brain cortex action. We can therefore anticipate that the better able we are to engage our cortex (thinking brain) when we feel anxiety or fear, the more likely we are to switch our brain to purple brain and have courage triumph over fear.

Further research needs to be done but, if this is true, it makes a case for the argument that when under high stress we have two options. We can go down the red-brain fear pathway of freeze or flight and do nothing or avoid/retreat from the threat. Or we can go down the purple brain pathway of courage, engage our full brain and move into assertive action, confronting the threat head-on including the cortex or thinking brain.

> *'Courage doesn't mean you don't get afraid,*
> *it means you don't let the fear stop you.'*
> — *Bethany Hamilton*

Courage is fear combined with the hope or mindset that your actions can make a difference. It is this mindset that leads to the fear being overtaken by courage. In a state of courage your normal fears of pain, injury and loss are inhibited through your focus on a higher purpose or goal. It's also possible for anger to prompt courage by similarly overriding fear. For example, I have heard of a phobic man who was only able to leave the house when he was angry with his wife. As soon as his anger subsided the fear returned and he had to go back home.

Purple brain and resilience

Some researchers say that certain people are simply more wired to be fearful and that others are more wired to be courageous. There is some truth in this but it isn't the full story. The brain is very plastic and neural pathways can be changed through practice, which means courage can be trained just like any other skill. This isn't anything new; the training of courage has been practised extensively throughout history. Courage has always been a universally admired virtue and throughout most of history courage was rated much more highly than comfort. In traditions all over the world, courage is trained by purposefully inducing discomfort. By learning to tolerate discomfort and pain, and go in pursuit of their goal in spite of it, people were effectively training their brain to gain control over their xiphoid nucleus and wiring it to activate purple brain over red brain. You could say that stress was used as a tool to train the brain, to activate the courageous purple brain instead of the 'cowardly' red brain.

Courage training is still done by some people — just think about military training or people climbing mountains, hiking through the rainforest or even going camping. Why would they voluntarily expose themselves to this kind of needless discomfort? The reason is that there is something very rewarding about facing your fears, tolerating discomforts and pushing your limits. The training of courage changes your mindset, builds mental strength and makes you more resilient.

One way it does this is through changing what is called the locus of control. Facing your fears and learning to tolerate discomfort makes people realize they don't have to be a product of their environment, and they begin to internalize what we call an internal locus of control. An internal locus of control is the belief that you can control the outcome of events through conscious effort. An external locus of control is the belief that your situation or circumstances determine the outcome and you have very little influence over them. It isn't hard to see how people with an internal locus of control tend to feel more confident, energized and are more likely to be successful.

WHICH IS YOUR LOCUS OF CONTROL?

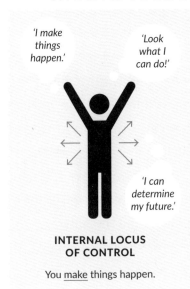

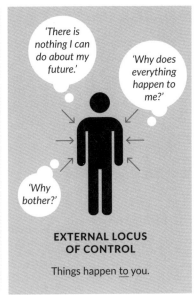

Internal locus of control

I determine the outcome

I have influence over things

If I don't like something I can change it

My environment is a product of my influence

External locus of control

The outcome depends on the situation

I have very little influence over things

If I don't like something there is little I can do about it

I am a product of my environment

How to train courage

Purposefully inducing discomfort might sound counterintuitive but given that discomfort grows resilience and an internal locus of control it might be worth it. Resilience combined with an internal locus of control create a mindset that is more likely to activate purple brain in the face of a challenge or threat because it influences how we assess the challenge. When you have small victories over difficult situations — small acts of courage that weren't pleasant in the moment but you made it through and the outcome was worth it — your courage mindset grows and you can take on bigger and bigger challenges. You are training your courage muscle and strengthening the courage pathways in your brain, making it easier and easier to act courageously. You are training yourself to activate purple brain over red brain when stress is high. You are getting better and better at keeping control through keeping your thinking brain engaged and allowing the empathy hormones to override the fear hormones.

I don't suggest we begin to self-inflict discomfort and challenges to grow courage. Rather I suggest we use our current challenges, both big and small, to train purple brain and grow in courage. We all have challenges and discomforts in our lives. They all offer us valuable training opportunities if we approach them with a courage mindset.

It is important to keep in mind that courage is not doing that which is *hard* but doing that which you *fear*. Discipline and courage are both important but they are not the same. To train courage you need to identify what scares you or intimidates you and then decide to do just that — or take small steps towards doing that. If you are afraid of public speaking, step up and volunteer to chair the next meeting you are in. If you are afraid of making mistakes, purposefully make three mistakes today. If you find it difficult to talk to people, commit to initiating a friendly chat with a new person each day. Success in these exercises is measured purely by completing the task, even if is was with trembling knees.

> *'You can choose courage or you can choose comfort, but you cannot choose both.'*
>
> — *Brené Brown*

Practising courage increases your capacity for courage, just like lifting weights increases the capacity of your muscles. If you lift dumbbells without any weight on them you are not challenging your system and its capacity won't grow. Some resistance or stress on the system is needed to generate growth. In order to practise courage you need two things. The first is a situation that triggers fear or stress in you — your dumbbell so to speak. Second, you need a courage mindset, a willingness to 'pick up the dumbbell' and put effort into using it to train your courage muscle.

In order to do this, your interpretation of the situation needs to be such that your brain can access purple brain in order to act courageously. If you interpret the situation as hard, painful or annoying, the amygdala system wins and you will want to avoid the situation. Then it becomes nothing but a strain on your system.

When you interpret the challenging situation as something you are willing to face and as a helpful opportunity for learning and growth, you are activating the cortex part of the xiphoid nucleus and the stress becomes the tool to growing courage.

For example:

» Running late can be frustrating and annoying (red brain) or it can be an opportunity to train yourself to manage stress under pressure (purple brain).

» When you have experienced a traumatic car crash, the fear of getting back into the car can be overwhelming and too hard (red brain) or it can be an opportunity to conquer your fear and rewire your brain (purple brain).

» Being yelled at by your manager can be scary and make you feel insecure (red brain) or it can be an opportunity to stand up for yourself and not tolerate unacceptable behaviour (purple brain).

When you activate a courage mindset that sees challenges and discomforts as opportunities for growth, you choose to activate purple brain over red brain and, in time, your brain will begin to rewire itself. You will be able to access purple-brain courage in situations you would never have been able to confront in the past.

Courage mindset and growth mindset

Carol S. Dweck, PhD is one of the world's leading researchers in the field of motivation and the originator of the theory of growth mindset. This is the belief that talent and capabilities are developed through effort and hard work, and that mistakes and setbacks offer valuable learning opportunities and are worth paying attention to. It's not surprising that Dweck found that a growth mindset is linked to heightened attention and full-brain activity when encountering difficult or challenging situations. For people with a growth mindset, all of the brain, including the cortex, becomes active when faced with a challenge (stress), which indicates that purple brain is activated.

The opposite of a growth mindset is a fixed mindset. People with a fixed mindset believe that talent and capabilities are set and not easily changed. For people with a fixed mindset, difficulties and mistakes are bad and painful experiences that they want to avoid. In people with a fixed mindset, challenges and discomforts are linked to decreased brain activity as they mentally avoid the difficulty.

People with a growth mindset interpret challenges as less threatening and therefore keep their forebrain engaged, enhancing brain activity which in turn improves learning, growth and achievements. Essentially, growth mindset and courage mindset tap into the same constructs and brain activity.

The purple-brain balancing act

I sometimes think of courage as a see-saw or balancing act. When you focus on the risks and the losses you could suffer from courageous action, you tip into red-brain fear and it becomes tempting to give up (flight or freeze response). When you focus on the things, people or situations that are causing the threat, you tip into red-brain anger and are at risk of lashing out, attacking and burning your bridges (fight response). Courage is found when you find the balance — not ignoring the threats or what's at stake, but focusing on the higher goal that you are trying to achieve through your courageous action and *why* you are trying to achieve that.

Your *why* is a shortcut back to purple-brain balance. When you ask yourself *Why do I have this goal? Why does it matter to me?* you will find your balance and fuel your purple brain.

For example, one of my clients had spent many years studying to become an engineer. She had a high-ranking job as one of the few women in her field, earned a good salary and was building an impressive resume. Yet she was miserable at work, constantly mistreated, bullied and disrespected. Every attempt to address this had backfired and she didn't want to turn it into a legal dispute. When she focused on the losses she would experience from walking away from the job, she got scared and felt stuck. When she focused on the people who were mistreating her, she felt angry and resentful. For a long time, she went back and forth between these two red-brain states, see-sawing between the red-brain fear of losing her salary, damaging her career and losing her comfortable lifestyle and her red-brain anger towards the people, the company and the situations in which she was mistreated. She was stuck and it was a miserable place to be.

Her goal was to have a good work–life balance, a fulfilling career, to work in a team that appreciated her and to use her skills for a greater cause. Her *why* was 'because I want to be happy'. When she put her focus on her goal and her why, and started asking herself questions about how to reach her goal, the fear and the anger lessened and in time she worked up the courage to quit. Quitting her job and taking time off to figure out what she wants to do with her career and her life is one of the most courageous things she has ever done.

Another client received a diagnosis of terminal illness right after he retired after a successful career. He see-sawed back and forth between the red-brain fear of death, fear of leaving behind his family, fear of his children having to grow up without a father, and red-brain anger — anger with life, the injustice of his diagnosis, and irritation with the people he loved most over their concern with the mundane day-to-day things of life. The higher goal for him is to be more in green brain, to spend his time it being present, non-judgmental and enjoying it as much as possible. His why is because he wants to spend the time that he has left in the best possible way, to make precious memories and to 'die well'. Choosing to not give in to old habits of always being busy, choosing not to revert back to fear and irritation but to choose thoughts that are true and helpful, when being faced with such a challenge, is a courageous act.

As I write this chapter I am in a period of learning to be more courageous. I am working on a not-for-profit project that has the potential to change the status quo in an area I am passionate about and improve things that I think are an injustice. It is my passion project. But as with every passion project that serves a higher purpose there is the red-brain see-saw. When I focus on the magnitude of the project, the obstacles, the lack of resources and the huge mountain of work that it involves, I feel insecure, scared and in over my head. I want to run away and hide and pretend the whole thing doesn't exist. When I focus on the opposition, the pushback, the many many unpaid hours, the late nights and slow progress, I dip into red-brain anger and feelings of frustration and resentment. When I keep my eyes on the goal and the why, changing the lives of many people in a way that is possible, needed and long overdue, the fear and frustration subside and courage resurfaces. This gives energy and vision, and motivates me to stop wasting my time and energy on worries and frustrations but instead return to skilful and deliberate action and to keep going.

Rediscovering the power of courage and the freedom it brings to be able to live and live well, even when things seem to be falling apart or seem too challenging to continue, is profound. To be able to meet red-brain triggers with a purple-brain response is to not complain about or get frustrated with the people or situations that block you, challenge you and sometimes even hurt you. Taking these things in your stride and moving forward with determination, focus and energy is what happens when you activate the state of courage. With green brain for our everyday lives, enjoying the present moment and recognizing and stopping needless and pointless worrying and stress, and purple brain for tackling our real challenges and discomforts, we will grow in present-moment happiness for when things are going well and courage and resilience for when things are not going according to plan.

Could courage, despite its need for discomforts and challenges, also be linked to happiness? If courage and happiness are linked this could be quite mind-blowing. It could mean that we in the West have been looking for happiness in the wrong place and have mistaken *comfort* for *happiness*. If this is true, shielding ourselves and our children from discomfort could in the long run make us and them unhappier. Which could explain why our increasing levels of comfort don't make our experienced happiness increase and why, despite the high levels of comfort in much of the western world, mental-health issues are on the rise. When we try so hard to eliminate discomfort, struggles and suffering from our lives and make laws to prevent us from even being offended, could it be that we are sacrificing our internal locus of control, courage, resilience and mental health in the process?

After experiencing the rewards that come from training a courage mindset and taking courageous action, I believe that purple brain could hold the key to greater mental health, mental strength and happiness that goes far beyond comfort.

EXERCISE 13:
HOW DO YOU ACTIVATE PURPLE BRAIN?

STEP 1. Identify a situation that you will use to practise purple-brain activation — something that causes you mild to strong stress, fear or anxiety.

_____

_____

STEP 2. Mindfully picture this situation while monitoring your breathing and muscle tension and placing one hand on your chest and one on your abdomen (this helps keep you out of red brain).

STEP 3. Create a courage mindset regarding this situation by answering these questions:

» What would the best possible outcome be?

» Why is this important to me?

» Which of my values does this connect to?

STEP 4. Ask yourself, 'What does courage look like for me in this situation?' Then notice what comes to mind without trying to change it or argue with it. Just observe with kindness.

_____

_____

_____

STEP 5. Ask yourself, 'What is the first step I can commit to?' Again, notice with kindness what comes to mind.

_____

_____

_____

CHAPTER 14:

Self-compassion

One of the most profound skills that mindfulness practice has taught me is self-compassion. I have never before felt so comfortable with being kind and considerate towards myself. Historically when I entered the red or orange brain, my inner critic always showed up with a loud voice. Calming it down, making room for a more positive and supportive voice, felt very counterintuitive, as if I were letting myself off the hook and would turn into a lazy, unproductive, irresponsible person.

My inner critic is not very nice. It is harsh, judgmental, angry, always doubting my abilities, mean and destructive. My inner critic would say things like:

> » What's wrong with you? You idiot! Why can't you just get it right?
> » You are such an impatient and horrible mother.
> » You are ugly and you definitely can't pull off wearing that dress.
> » You have to work harder and get this done.
> » They won't help you or back you up.

To put it simply, my inner critic is a jerk.

I would never, ever talk to anyone else this way, yet I felt totally okay and comfortable talking to myself this way every single day. Before I started to practise mindfulness I never questioned this inner voice; instead I just accepted its chatter in my mind. Letting go of it felt surprisingly scary and unsafe, like I was forfeiting control, as if I were letting myself loose in a candy shop to eat all the candy without paying for it.

Most of us are able to identify with having an inner critic, and know it usually shows up when we are in the red zone. But why does it even exist? There is not one answer to this question; instead there are several contributors.

Childhood experiences

Childhood experiences are never all bad or all good, but the negative ones seem to echo through in the voice of the inner critic. Often the things our inner critic says resemble correcting messages we received either implicitly or explicitly from our caregivers or how they made us feel. It all starts with the way a young child's brain works: it always perceives what the caregivers say as true and accurate.

For example, when a stressed-out father yells at his four-year-old son and tells him he is 'a disgusting boy', the child's brain is unable to see that actually he is just a child and that his father is the one acting in a disgusting way. The child accepts and believes what he is told. If this pattern is repeated on a regular basis, it is likely that the developing inner critic starts to use similar phrases.

When a young child consistently hears the message *you are the oldest so you should be (more) responsible*, this can lead to an inner voice that reminds the person that they are responsible for other people's behaviour and happiness, that they should know better, do better and not be so selfish.

If the message was *you are not as smart as your sister*, the inner-voice criticism might focus on commenting on a lack of abilities and skills.

If the message was *boys don't cry*, the inner critic is likely to tell the person to keep vulnerable emotions under control with thoughts like *you can't be weak.*

Attachment

Attachment theory is a psychological model that was first described by psychologist, psychiatrist and psychoanalyst John Bowlby. Attachment theory describes the relationship between two humans, although the term 'attachment' is most often used to describe the relationship between a child and their caregiver. Essentially it describes the ability of a person to develop basic trust in their caregiver and consequently in themselves and others.

There are three forms of attachment: secure attachment, insecure attachment and avoidant attachment.

Secure attachment develops when the caregiver is available and responsive to the child's needs. A child who is securely attached to a caregiver feels safe, accepted and free to explore and make mistakes, because they trust that their caregiver will be there for them in times of need. They have a safe base to return to when things go wrong. This is a state of green brain.

Insecure attachment (or ambivalent attachment) will develop when the caregiver is unpredictably or conditionally responsive to the child's needs. A child who is insecurely attached is more likely to feel angry, anxious or ambivalent in relationships and will have a tendency to both seek and resist contact. This has strong links to orange brain — *I am okay as long as I am* ... [conditions of the caregiver are met].

Avoidant attachment develops when the caregiver consistently does not respond to the needs of the child. A child with avoidant attachment avoids disappointment and upset by no longer seeking closeness. They stay close enough to the parent to maintain protection but distant enough to avoid rejection. They will have strong underlying emotions such as sadness and fear.

The nature of your relationship with your primary caregiver shapes the way you relate to yourself. You can experience secure attachment to yourself, insecure attachment and even avoidant attachment.

Someone with a secure attachment style is likely to feel capable, confident and able to relate to themselves in a kind and supportive way. They trust themselves and have a safe internal world. Their core beliefs will be along the lines of:

» *I am okay as I am.*
» *I can cope.*
» *The world is safe to explore.*
» *I am supported.*

Someone with an insecure attachment style is likely to only conditionally accept themselves, in a way that resembles the messages they received from their caregiver. For example:

» *I am okay as long as I work hard/take care of others/am found attractive/others are happy.*
» *I have to . . .*
» *The world is safe as long as I . . .*
» *I am supported as long as I . . .*

Someone with an avoidant attachment style is likely to be judgmental, harsh and unsupportive towards themselves. Their underlying core beliefs are likely to be something along these lines:

» *I am not okay.*

» *I have to protect myself.*

» *The world is not safe.*

» *I am alone.*

INSIGHT INSPIRATION

Is your self-talk mostly negative, neutral or positive?

1. Write down some of your negative self-talk. (This can be confronting and you might feel inclined to skip this step, but it is very helpful to know your negative self-talk so you can effectively change it.)

   _____

   _____

   _____

   _____

2. Given your past experiences, why does it make perfect sense that you would have these thoughts about yourself? ('Because they are true' is not the right answer!)

   _____

   _____

   _____

   _____

The social brain

We all have attachment experiences and styles that have shaped the social structures of our brain and therefore shape how we feel about others, the world and ourselves. Studies show that mindfulness practice activates and reshapes these social structures. Because of neuroplasticity, practising mindfulness or any of the other green-brain techniques on a regular basis leads to stronger social circuits in the brain that become more easily activated. You could say that practising mindfulness on a regular basis reshapes the social structures in your brain into a more secure attachment structure.

As Daniel Siegel puts it:

> 'Mindfulness is not only a form of attention training and it is not only a form of affect regulation training. Mindfulness is a relational process where you become your own best friend.'

How to grow a kinder inner voice

All of the green-brain techniques soften old constructs that dictate how we see and relate to ourselves. This process opens up the way for developing a kinder inner voice. When thoughts like *you idiot, you are never going to succeed* or *no one really cares about you* come up, there are various techniques you can use.

1. Stop responding

One way of approaching a self-critical thought is by noticing it without engaging with it or responding to it; a thought is just a thought unless you believe it and engage with it. Then gently and kindly turn your attention back to your breath, your senses or whatever it is that you are doing. This way you don't give the thought any power or control. In time the unhelpful thought will come up less and less because you are not reinforcing it.

2. Befriend the inner critic

One way to calm your critical inner voice is by actually 'befriending' it. Try to be curious about what is triggering it without believing everything it says. This helps the healthy adult part of you to stay in control while you find out what underlying hurt is triggered so you can address that. You can apply the ALL technique (see page 70) for this.

'Angry is just sad's bodyguard.'

— *Liza Palmer*

3. Mantra

When you practise a kind and supportive mantra regularly, you will be surprised at how quickly your inner voice becomes kinder. You can use the helpful, green-brain thoughts that come up when you go through the ALL process and turn them into a mantra for that period, or you can use the affirmations discussed in Chapter 7. It does not matter what you use as long as the thoughts are positive and kind and you practise them on a regular basis.

Back yourself up, instead of beating yourself up

Learning to back yourself up with kind, compassionate self-talk, instead of beating yourself up with harsh and critical self-talk, will eliminate one of your most powerful red-brain triggers and drastically increase green-brain activity.

My mean, self-critical voice still shows up every now and then. When it does I can see it for what it is and gently and kindly turn my focus back to thoughts that are actually helpful to me in that moment. When the feeling that I constantly need to learn, grow and achieve more all the time creeps back in — you might call it perfectionism — I remind myself that a state of being present and content with where I am at will be more effective in reaching my goals. To remind me of this, I have a mantra sitting on my desk that says: You are exactly where you need to be.

The underlying truth is that I am okay just as I am in this moment. Every time I read this mantra I am reminded of this truth and it calms my rushing tendencies and activates my green brain. Then in that green-brain state I am much more effective and efficient in working towards my goals in a sustainable and fun way.

 RENEW YOUR MIND TIP

For a quick boost in self-compassion, place one hand on your chest and one hand on your stomach. This resembles giving yourself an encouraging hug. Your brain will respond by activating the social engagement system and releasing oxytocin.

Concluding thoughts

I hope you have enjoyed this book, but most of all I hope that it has helped you realize the value of cultivating your green and purple brain.

In the beginning of the book I asked you to imagine you could navigate your everyday life with a mind that is calm and focused and face your biggest challenges filled with courage and positive thoughts. What would be different?

If you have tried out the techniques in this book you will have experienced the powerful effect of renewing your mind and training your brain. You will have had moments or even days of living what you have imagined when you started out on this journey. But I need to warn you: you will only experience lasting effects if you are able to keep using these techniques on a regular basis. They don't work as an operation after which you are 'fixed'; rather, they work as brain vitamins. Without a good dose of vitamins on a regular, ideally daily, basis the effects wear off. The people who will get the most out of this book and find it truly life-changing are those who use it this way. Those who keep it to hand and who re-read chapters based on what is happening in their lives — and, most importantly, take the time to implement and practise the skills — will reap the green- and purple-brain rewards.

This disclaimer also applies to me. Even though I know the techniques and content of this book inside out, without ongoing practice I too will revert back to orange and red brain when under stress. *Knowing* isn't enough; it's the *doing* that counts.

Whenever I feel stressed, irritated, sad or insecure I use these emotions as a reminder to practise the Renew Your Mind techniques. They are a signal that I have left the green zone and they prompt me to use the techniques in my toolbox to get back to green. The techniques or variations that will work best depend on your situation and personal preference.

To renew your mind and live everyday life from the green brain, you don't necessarily need to master all of the techniques. They are all designed to bring you back to green but they use different routes to accomplish this. As long as you have one or two well-trodden pathways back to green, that's what matters most. For those big challenges that seem hard to crack, you have purple-brain courage available to you to keep your brain out of fear and able to rise to the occasion.

Too many people spend their days feeling stressed, anxious or depressed, giving in to fear instead of moving into courage, damaging their health, relationships and happiness in the process. We only have one life. The day-to-day things may not seem significant but days become weeks, weeks become months, months become years, and years turn into decades. To live life to the fullest we need to start with the day-to-day things. Every time you choose green over orange or red brain, every moment of courage and kindness matters. Those moments, no matter how small or insignificant they may seem, combine to make a huge difference.

The secret to a happy and successful life is not just hard work or circumstance; it is being in control of your brain by being in control of your thoughts. Retraining your brain to reduce stress and activate green brain is free and can be done any time and anywhere.

If you apply science to taking care of your brain, if you get past the productivity myth, train your brain to stay in green, and access purple when facing a challenge, then you haven't only renewed your mind but you've also renewed your life.

Let me leave you with this story:

An old Cherokee told his grandson:

'There is a battle between two wolves inside us all. One is evil. It is anger, jealousy, greed, resentment, inferiority, lies and ego. The other is good. It is joy, peace, love, hope, humility, kindness, empathy and truth.'

The boy thought about it and asked,

'Grandfather, which wolf wins?'

The old man quietly replied, 'The one you feed.'

— Unknown

References

Chapter 2

Kathryn Birnie, Michael Speca and Linda E. Carlson, 'Exploring self-compassion and empathy in the context of mindfulness-based stress reduction (MBSR)', *Stress and Health*, December 2010.

Sarah Bowen, Katie Witkiewitz, Tiara M. Dillworth, Neharika Chawla, Tracy L. Simpson, Brian D. Ostafin, Mary E. Larimer, Arthur W. Blume, George A. Parks and G. Alan Marlatt, 'Mindfulness meditation and substance use in an incarcerated population', *Psychology of Addictive Behaviors*, September 2006.

Richard J. Davidson, Jon Kabat-Zinn, Jessica Schumacher, Melissa Rosenkranz, Daniel Muller, Saki F. Santorelli, Ferris Urbanowski, Anne Harrington, Katherine Bonus and John F. Sheridan, 'Alterations in brain and immune function produced by mindfulness meditation', *Psychosomatic Medicine*, July 2003.

Ian Donald, Paul Taylor, Sheena Johnson, Cary Cooper, Susan Cartwright and Susannah Robertson, 'Work environments, stress, and productivity: An examination using ASSET', *International Journal of Stress Management*, November 2005.

Norman A.S. Farb, Adam K. Anderson and Zindel V. Segal, 'The mindful brain and emotion regulation in mood disorders', *Canadian Journal of Psychiatry*, February 2012.

Paul Grossman, Ludger Niemann, Stefan Schmidt and Harald Walach, 'Mindfulness-based stress reduction and health benefits: A meta-analysis', *Journal of Psychosomatic Research*, July 2004.

Stefan G. Hofmann, Alice T. Sawyer, Ashley A. Witt and Diana Oh, 'The effect of mindfulness-based therapy on anxiety and depression: A meta-analytic review', *Journal of Consulting and Clinical Psychology*, April 2010.

Phan Y. Hong, David A. Lishner, Kim H. Han, Elizabeth A. Huss, 'The positive impact of mindful eating on expectations of food liking', *Mindfulness*, June 2011.

J.W. Hughes, D.M. Fresco, R. Myerscough, M.H. van Dulmen, L.E. Carlson and R. Josephson, 'Randomized controlled trial of mindfulness-based stress reduction for prehypertension', *Psychosomatic Medicine*, October 2013.

Ute R. Hülsheger, Hugo J.E.M. Alberts, Alina Feinholdt and Jonas W.B. Lang, 'Benefits of mindfulness at work: The role of mindfulness in emotion regulation, emotional exhaustion, and job satisfaction', *Journal of Applied Psychology*, March 2013.

Itai Ivtzan, Hanna E. Gardner and Zhanar Smailova, 'Mindfulness meditation and curiosity: The contributing factors to wellbeing and the process of closing the self-discrepancy gap', *International Journal of Wellbeing*, 2011.

Shamini Jain, Shauna L. Shapiro, Summer Swanick, Scott C. Roesch, Paul J. Mills, Iris Bell and Gary E.R. Schwartz, 'A randomized controlled trial of mindfulness meditation versus relaxation training: Effects on distress, positive states of mind, rumination, and distraction', *Annals of Behavioral Medicine*, February 2007.

Muhammad Jamal, 'Job stress and job performance controversy: An empirical assessment', *Organizational Behavior and Human Performance*, February 1984.

Shian-Ling Keng, Moria J. Smoski and Clive J. Robins, 'Effects of mindfulness on psychological health: A review of empirical studies', *Clinical Psychology Review*, August 2011.

Cara Murphy and James MacKillop, 'Living in the here and now: Interrelationships between impulsivity, mindfulness, and alcohol misuse', *Psychopharmacology*, January 2012.

Esther K. Papies, Lawrence W. Barsalou and Ruud Custers, 'Mindful attention prevents mindless impulses', *Social Psychological and Personality Science*, May 2012.

Shauna L. Shapiro, Gary E. Schwartz and Ginny Bonner, 'Effects of mindfulness-based stress reduction on medical and premedical students', *Journal of Behavioral Medicine*, December 1998.

Bruce W. Smith, Alexis J. Ortiz, Laurie E. Steffen, Erin M. Tooley, Kathryn T. Wiggins, Elizabeth A. Yeater, John D. Montoya and Michael L. Bernard, 'Mindfulness is associated with fewer PTSD symptoms, depressive symptoms, physical symptoms, and alcohol problems in urban firefighters', *Journal of Consulting and Clinical Psychology*, October 2011.

Mark A. Runco, *Creativity: Theories and Themes: Research, Development, and Practice*, Elsevier, 2014.

J.M.G. Williams, Y. Alatiq, C. Crane, T. Barnhofer, M.J.V. Fennell, D.S. Duggan, S. Hepburn and G.M. Goodwin, 'Mindfulness-based Cognitive Therapy (MBCT) in bipolar disorder: Preliminary evaluation of immediate effects on between-episode functioning', *Journal of Affective Disorders*, April 2008.

Chapter 3

Stephen W. Porges, 'The polyvagal theory: Phylogenetic substrates of a social nervous system', *International Journal of Psychophysiology*, October 2001.

Chapter 5

Abiola Keller, Kristin Litzelman, Lauren E. Wisk, Torsheika Maddox, Erika Rose Cheng, Paul D. Creswell and Whitney P. Witt, 'Does the perception that stress affects health matter? The association with health and mortality', *Health Psychology*, September 2012.

J.P. Jamieson, M.K. Nock and W.B. Mendes, 'Mind over matter: Reappraising arousal improves cardiovascular and cognitive responses to stress', *Journal of Experimental Psychology: General*, August 2012.

Chapter 7

Barbara L. Fredrickson, 'The broaden–and–build theory of positive emotions', *Philosophical Transactions of the Royal Society B: Biological Sciences*, September 2004.

Chapter 8

Sian L. Beilock and Rob Gray, 'From attentional control to attentional spillover: A skill-level investigation of attention, movement, and performance outcomes', *Human Movement Science*, December 2012.

Amy J.C. Cuddy, Caroline A. Wilmuth and Dana R. Carney, 'The benefit of power posing before a high-stakes social evaluation', Harvard Business School Working Paper, September 2012.

Susan Goldin-Meadow and Sian L. Beilock, 'Action's influence on thought: The case of gesture', *Perspectives on Psychological Science*, November 2010.

Carly Kontra, Susan Goldin-Meadow and Sian L. Beilock, 'Embodied learning across the life span', *Topics in Cognitive Science*, October 2012.

M.A. Wollmer, C. de Boer, N. Kalak, J. Beck, T. Götz, T. Schmidt, M. Hodzic, U. Bayer, T. Kollman, K. Kollewe, D. Sonmez, K. Duntsch, M.D. Haug, M. Schedlowski, M. Hatzinger, D. Dressler, S. Brand, E. Holsboer-Trachsler and T.H. Kruger, 'Facing depression with botulinum toxin: A randomized controlled trial', *Journal of Psychiatric Research*, May 2012.

Chapter 9

Bruno S. Frey and Alois Stutzer, 'Happiness research: State and prospects', *Review of Social Economy*, June 2005.

Richard M. Ryan and Edward L. Deci, 'On happiness and human potentials: A review of research on hedonic and eudaimonic well-being', *Annual Review of Psychology*, February 2001.

Chapter 10

Richard Wiseman, *The Luck Factor*, Random House, 2011.

Chapter 11

Sara B. Algoe and Baldwin Way, 'Evidence for a role of the oxytocin system, indexed by genetic variation in CD38, in the social bonding effects of expressed gratitude', *Social Cognitive and Affective Neuroscience*, January 2014.

Michael Babyak, James A. Blumenthal, Steve Herman, Parinda Khatri, Murali Doraiswamy, Kathleen Moore, Edward Craighead, Tei T. Baldewicz and Krishnan K. Ranga, 'Exercise treatment for major depression: Maintenance of therapeutic benefit at 10 months', *Psychosomatic Medicine*, September/October 2000.

Margaret M. Bass, Catherine A. Duchowny, Maria M. Llabre, 'The effect of therapeutic horseback riding on social functioning in children with autism', *Journal of Autism and Developmental Disorders*, September 2009.

Marian R. Banks and William A. Banks, 'The effects of animal-assisted therapy on loneliness in an elderly population in long-term care facilities, *The Journals of Gerontology: Series A*, December 2001.

Andrea Beetz, Kerstin Uvnäs-Moberg, Henri Julius and Kurt Kotrschal, 'Psychosocial and psychophysiological effects of human–animal interactions: The possible role of oxytocin', *Frontiers in Psychology*, 2012.

Adam J. Guastella, Philip B. Mitchell and Mark R. Dadds, 'Oxytocin increases gaze to the eye region of human faces', *Biological Psychiatry*, January 2008.

Kristiann C. Heesch, Yolanda R. van Gellecum, Nicola W. Burton, Jannique G.Z. van Uffelen and Wendy J. Brown, 'Physical activity, walking, and quality of life in women with depressive symptoms', *American Journal of Preventive Medicine*, January 2015.

J. Holt-Lunstad, T.B. Smith and J.B. Layton, 'Social relationships and mortality risk: A meta-analytic review', *PLOS Medicine*, July 2010.

Michael W. Kraus, Cassy Huang and Dacher Keltner, 'Tactile communication, cooperation, and performance: An ethological study of the NBA', *EMOTION*, October 2010.

Egil W. Martinsen, A. Medhus and L. Sandvik, 'Effects of aerobic exercise on depression: A controlled study', *British Medical Journal*, July 1985.

Murray B. Stein, 'Sweating away the blues: Can exercise treat depression?', *American Journal of Preventive Medicine*, January 2005.

Kevin Wheldall, Kate Bevan and Kath Shortall, 'A touch of reinforcement: The effects of contingent teacher touch on the classroom behaviour of young children', *Educational Review*, 1986.

P.J. Zak, A.A. Stanton and S. Ahmadi, 'Oxytocin increases generosity in humans', *PLOS ONE*, November 2007.

Chapter 13

Cynthia L.S. Pury, and Shane J. Lopez, *The Psychology of Courage: Modern research on an ancient virtue*, Amer Psychological Association, 2010

Kelly McGonigal, *The Upside of Stress: Why stress is good for you, and how to get good at it*, Avery, 2015

Uri Nili, Hagar Goldberg, Abraham Weizman and Yadin Duda, 'Fear thou not: Activity of frontal and temporal circuits in moments of real-life courage, *Neuron*, June 2010

Chapter 14

Karen Goodall, Anna Trejnowska and Stephen Darling, 'The relationship between dispositional mindfulness, attachment security and emotion regulation', *Personality and Individual Differences*, April 2012.

Daniel J. Siegel, 'Mindful awareness, mindsight, and neural integration, *The Humanistic Psychologist*, June 2009.

Index